HEDGE WITCH

AND THE ART OF HEDGE RIDING

BY

RACHEL PATTERSON

PUBLISHED BY Fenix Flames Publishing Ltd 2024

Copyright © 2024 Rachel Patterson

All rights reserved including the right of reproduction in whole or in part in any form. No reproduction, copy or transmission of this publication may be made without written permission. No paragraph of this publication may be reproduced, copied or transmitted save with written permission or in accordance with the provisions of the Copyright Act 1956 (as amended). Any person who performs any unauthorised act in relation to this publication may be liable to criminal prosecution and civil claims for damages. The moral rights of the author have been asserted.

All names have been changed, except in those cases where individuals are already publicly known.

Published by Fenix Flames Publishing Ltd

Design & Layout: Ben Rees

Printed by Lightning Source International / Ingram Spark

Paperback ISBN 978-1-913768-20-1
ebook ISBN 978-1-913768-21-8

www.publishing.fenixflames.co.uk

CONTENTS

Introduction xi

1. What is the Craft? 1
2. Where do you work your magic? ... 3
3. What's in the name? 5
4. Boundaries and liminal places 9
5. Connection and spirit of place 11
6. Hedge Riding 15
7. How do you get there? 17
8. State of mind 23
9. States of conscious 25
10. Our Minds 27
- Your conscious mind, your middle self 27
- The psychic mind, your lower self, your younger self 28
- The Divine mind, the higher self, the older self 28

11. The Three Worlds 31
12. The Nine Worlds 33
13. Breath work 35
14. Visualisation 37
15. Sheilds up! 41
16. Grounding 43
17. Chants 45
18. Smudging 51
19. The spoken word 55
20. Offerings 57
21. Staff, stand and besom 59
22. Journey bag 63
23. Spirits of all kinds 67
24. The Fair Folk 71
25. The Gods 73
26. Preparation 75
27. Ritual 77
- Hallowing the Compass 77
- Treading the Mill 87
28. Hedge Riding Guardian 91
29. Entering the Otherworld 93
30. Magical herbs 99

- Harvesting 102
- Charging 106
- Simples 107
- Oils 107
- Incense 111
- Herb bundles 113
- Mists 114
- Potions 115

31. Into the Hedge 119
32. Flying Ointment 135
33. Hedge Riding Herbal Tea 147
34. Hedge Riding candle 149
35. Crystals 151
36. Park your broomstick 163

Recommended reading 165
About the author 167

Disclaimer

If you have ailments or mental health issues, get them diagnosed by a medical professional. If it is advised, work out a course of medication. This book does not in any way replace the need for proper medical treatment, including medication or therapy for mental health issues. I do not advocate self-diagnosis. Always seek professional advice.

Never self-medicate, even with herbal remedies. Herbal remedies can be extremely potent; some are toxic. Others can react with prescription or over-the-counter medications in adverse ways. Please do not ingest any herbs if you aren't sure, you have identified them correctly. If you are on medication or have health issues, please do not ingest any herbs without first consulting a qualified practitioner.

Introduction

¹The discoverie
of witchcraft,
Wherein the lewde dealing of witches
and witchmongers is notablie detected, the
knaverie of coniurors, the impietie of inchan-
tors, the follie of toothſaiers, the impudent falſ-
hood of couſenors, the infidelitie of atheiſts,
the peſtilent practiſes of Pythoniſts, the
curioſitie of figurecaſters, the va-
nitie of dreamers, the beggerlie
art of Alcu-
myſtrie,
The abhomination of idolatrie, the horrible art of poiſoning, the vertue and power of
naturall magike, and all the conueiances
of Legierdemaine and iuggling are deciphered:
and many other things opened, which
have long lien hidden, howbeit

verie necessarie to
be knowne.
Heerevnto is added a treatiſe upon the
nature and ſubſtance of spirits and diuels,

&c: all latelie written
by Reginald Scot
Esquire.

---

1   The Discoverie of Witchcraft, Reginald Scott, 1584

My journey as a Pagan Witch began many years ago. My pathway has twisted and turned over the decades with me picking up things that worked and discarding those practices that don't. My journey is personal to me but what it does include is a lot of folk magic, kitchen witchcraft and of course, the art of the hedge witch. Some areas of the practice will work for you, others not so much, this is your journey so make it your own.

When I looked at writing this book it was primarily because people were asking me about hedge riding, which for me is a key part of being a Hedge Witch. The clue is in the name. And although I believe that riding the hedge is an integral part of being a Hedge Witch there is more to the pathway, some of which I hope to share with you in this book.

Do I live in a tumble-down cottage on the edge of a forest, with woodland creatures to help with the housework and a kitchen full of jars with weird and unidentifiable contents foraged from the hedgerows? Um...no. I live in a terraced house, albeit old (it was built in 1910), it is on the edge, but the edge of a large city. I do have the bonus that I only live a five-minute drive away from the ocean in one direction and the woods in the other direction though. However, local parks and city hedgerows do offer lots of plants and weeds that can be foraged and use for magic, as well as all the items I grow in my little garden. I do have a collection of jars filled with weird, dried herbs and plants along with a few bones, broken mirror pieces and other slightly dubious contents. As for the woodland creatures?

We do get foxes, pigeons, sparrows, magpies and the odd seagull in the garden but it is hard enough getting our human teenager to load the dishwasher let alone training the wildlife to help out. Basically, what I am saying, is that anyone can be a Witch, and anyone can practice Hedge Witchcraft no matter what your situation. Everything can be adapted to work for you. It is your pathway, make it your own.

I have lived on a farm in the country in the middle of nowhere, I have lived in a village, a town and now a city. They all have their own unique energies, pros and cons.

I like to bring my Kitchen Witchcraft into my practice, and I believe it works hand in hand with Hedge Witchcraft. Using ingredients from the kitchen cupboards in tandem with things I have foraged or brought in from the garden to work magic. My Craft also includes working magic with whatever I have to hand whether it is herbs from the garden, a feather found on a walk or a dog poop bag from my pocket, magic is everywhere.

My own spiritual pathway is Pagan, I work with the old gods, primarily ancient English ones but have worked with deities from across the globe over the years. You don't need to work with the gods, it is your choice to do so, or not.

I work, I am a wife, a mother, the obedient servant to a fussy dachshund and a human being with all the usual mundane life stuff going on. My craft and my magic need to fit into my everyday life, I live and work as a Witch, they are not separate things.

Whilst I do run an online school of witchcraft, an online coven and various online events along with my Kitchen Witch team, a lot of my witchcraft practice is worked as a solitary. I believe I have the best of both worlds, a coven and community when I need it, but the option to fly solo should I wish to. Again, it is your pathway, make it work for you.

Rachel Patterson
2024

1
What is the craft?

The term Witchcraft covers a magical practice but not just one straightforward structure, it is an umbrella term for all kinds of pathways. Witchcraft and Paganism in general are often linked with the idea that at the base of it all is nature. I do think this is correct in some form, we all work with nature in certain ways, and we use it as a connection. But Witchcraft is so much more, particularly the pathway of a Hedge Witch. We do connect with the natural world, the planet and all that lives on it. What a Witch does is to connect to the power of the universe, delving into the mysteries of the worlds and other realms and learning about and working with the cycles of life, death and rebirth. A Witch learns how to connect with those powers and to learn the wisdom and knowledge that comes with it. We tap into those powers and learn those mysteries to enable us to grow. Those powers are forms of energy that we connect with often in the form of Gods or deities of some kind. We do not always know or give them names they might just be the Lord and Lady or Father Sky and Mother Earth. It could be that you are more comfortable just working with the spirit of the land, the sea and the forests. There is no right or wrong here. My own personal view is this; in the beginning there was a spirit, an energy form and it was both male and female and also neither.

As spirituality spread down to the world each culture interpreted it in their own way, creating their own religion and singular or multiple deities. I see this main energy as the goddess, she is a huge diamond and each of the individual gods and goddesses are facets of that one diamond. Each one has its own unique personality and characteristics but ultimately, they are all part of the whole. I do work with individual deities, and I tend to stick to English and occasionally British deities because that works for me. But I also use general terms such as 'the goddess' and 'the god'. Do what works for you. I like working with a balance for the most part with a male and a female energy, but I do lean towards working more with the Goddess. What I would encourage you to do is research the deities, legends and myths for your local areas.

2
Where do you work your magic?

If we lived in a world of fairy tales then a witch would probably ride the hedge, hallow the compass, tread the mill and all the other wonderful magical things outside in nature. Perhaps in a grove of trees or standing in the middle of open moorland (sigh...how I wish). In reality most of us live in urban settings and whilst it is possible to take ourselves off to woods, fields or seashores, sometimes it is not possible or safe to do so on our own. If you can, then go for it, because nature is a truly wonderful place to work magic. But there are other options. I live on the edge of a city, but I have a small walled garden and it is a wonderful setting to work magic in. Not just because it is full of nature but because it is also imbued with my energy. I have worked the land, grown the plants and fed and watered it all, which gives me a very strong connection to the land. However, I have also worked magic of all kinds and been on incredible hedge riding journeys indoors in my kitchen, my spare room and my bedroom. Do not let the landscape and the venue restrict you.

3
What's in the name?

I have always been led to understand that being a Hedge Witch meant you walked between the worlds with one foot in this reality and another 'over the hedge' in the Otherworld. However, it seems more recently the name of Hedge Witch has come to refer to a solitary witch. Here are my suggestions on what being a Hedge Witch covers:

- Is practised by solitary witches
- Works with the Otherworld, spirit work and shamanic practices, riding the hedge
- Involves the study of plants and nature
- Is reminiscent of the ancient cunning folk and wise men and women who lived on the outskirts of society
- Magic is intertwined into daily life and mundane chores
- Works with the herbal world for remedies and spell working
- Works with the spirit of the land
- Connects with the spirit of the plants
- Connects with the spirit of animals
- Keeps the magical practice simple and uncomplicated
- Living and working in tune with nature and the seasons
- Has seer abilities
- Uses shamanic and seiðr practices

Whilst the tern 'hedge witch' does seem to be a modern one, the practise that it covers is very old. [1]There is some suggestion the term 'hedge rider' derives from the Saxon word 'haegtessa', the idea being the cunning folk lived on the outskirts of the town, literally the 'other side of the hedge' between the towns and the wilderness. This also being represented by the cunning folk being able to walk between the worlds, riding the hedge to the Otherworld.

I have done a bit of research on the etymology, and this is what I found. The suggestion that 'haegtessa' means 'hedge rider' can be found on various internet searches but they all seem to stem back to the books by Rae Beth[2]. The old English word 'hægtesse' seems to mean 'witch, sorceress, enchantress' or what we often see as the shortened version of 'hag'.

In Dutch 'heks' and German 'hexe' both mean 'witch'. The Old English word for hedge was 'hecg' or 'haga' in Dutch it would be 'heg'. In Old Norse we find the word ' tunriða' and Old High German 'zunritha', both which translate to 'hedge rider' which was used to refer to witches and ghosts. It is suggested the term 'hægtesse' could have referred at one time to those that gave prophecies or had oracular powers, later on it covered village wise women in general. Note this is interestingly a feminine version of the word with seemingly no masculine version, although I do believe there were male cunning folk. The term 'haga' also refers to the hawthorn tree.

In the 1500s it seems the hedge was poorly thought of and represented a place for 'vagabonds to shelter or resort' and to suggest some-

---

1   Rae Beth - https://knibbworld.com/
2   https://www.etymonline.com/

one was a 'hedge' anything was to imply they carried out their trade under a hedge because they were poor and of the lower class. It seems the term may have roots in history after all with slightly different meanings depending on which time period you look at.

With variations in meaning from hedge rider, witch, soothsayer, hag, healer, herbalist and of course, one who has a foot in both this world and the Otherworld. In Norse the term 'hægtesse' is sometimes used as an alternative term for the Norns, the three goddesses of Fate.

Hedge riding is very shamanic and incorporates the art of seiðr (pronounced "SAY-der") which is from old Norse. The word[1] seiðr translates to mean 'cord, string or snare'. It describes a form of magic and shamanic practice that involves working within the structure of fate to bring about changes. To do this the practitioner uses a ritual stick or spindle to 'weave' their goal by entering a trance state and interacting with the Otherworld.

Whatever the history of the term, it is now used to describe a wonderfully magical pathway.

---

[1] The Viking Spirit, Daniel McCoy

4
Boundaries and liminal places

Why the use of the word hedge? It is an in between region, a boundary between places and a magically liminal space[1]. In fields you will find a hedge marking the boundaries between other fields, trackways and woodlands. For the Hedge Witch the hedge is a boundary between our world and the Otherworld, a liminal space that leads into other realms. There are plenty of liminal places, those that are 'in between' not just physically but also spiritually and between worlds. One of my favourite liminal places is the shore where the ocean means the land. Doorways and gateways are also liminal spots. Anyone that is familiar with The Labyrinth film (and if you are not, why not?) will recognise the goblins stand in the doorways of Sarah's house. This is because doorways are a liminal place between our world and theirs. You might work with the idea of the World Tree or [2]Yggdrasil. Both of these are gateways or portals into the other worlds. Yggdrasil forms the centre of Norse spirituality providing an entryway into the nine worlds. The [3]World or Cosmic Tree can be found in many cultures and represents a connection between the heavens and the earth often providing a connection between our world and that of deity or the

---

1   of, relating to, or being an intermediate state, phase, or condition: IN-BETWEEN, TRANSITIONAL – Merriam Webster dictionary
2   https://norse-mythology.org/
3   Britannica.com

divine. The tree symbolism is important as it provides a recognisable image that we can usually all relate to, with branches stretching up into the skies, a solid trunk on the earth and roots that stretch down below the ground. A clear symbol to work easily with the upper, middle and underworlds.

5
Connection and spirit of place

What I do believe is absolutely necessary for a Hedge Witch, actually for any Witch if I am being honest, is a connection to the land you live on. I would stretch that to a connection to the energy of the land you live on, the seasons, the energy of the day and the spirit of the house you live in. It is all about connection. Every space, every place, every building no matter how ancient or modern has a living energy to it. The land beneath our feet holds onto memories and echoes of those that lived, worked and passed by there before you. Buildings hold onto the energy of those that lived or worked within its walls. To feel at home, to be part of the web of energy across the land and to successfully work magic you need to connect to that energy. The Romans referred to it as [1]Genius Loci or 'spirit of the place' and that term sums it up perfectly for me. They used the term when they were not sure of the name of the local or resident deity, but it has come to be used to refer to the spirit or energy of any place you are in.

I talk to my house; some may think I am totally bonkers for doing so (or just totally bonkers) but the house has stood for well over one hundred years and has accumulated a lot of energy. I believe it helps to let it know when we are going away, or

---

1   Dictionary of Roman Religion, L & R Adkins, 1996

when we are about to knock a wall down for renovations. It is about being connected to not only the house but the land it stands on. Whilst our house was built in 1910, there were houses here before that and in fact thousands of years before. The land in my area has had dwellings on since neolithic times. Imagine the history the piece of ground beneath my house has seen and felt? It holds the echoes of that history. Making and keeping that connection with my house and the land helps keep the energy in our home positive and gives a sense of belonging.

Whenever we hold rituals in fields, forests or wherever we might find ourselves on our wanderings, the first thing I do is connect with the energy of the land. I ask permission from the spirits of place and the ancestors there to allow us to perform our rite, and give an offering, usually a libation of some sort. It helps the ritual to run smoothly if you have made that connection.

If I am visiting somewhere, I love to connect with the energy of the place to get a feel for the history. Some places have stronger energies than others, be warned there are also some places that have overwhelming negative energies too. Be prepared. Once, many years ago when I was a fresh-faced witch I visited Hastings, we trekked out to the site of the famous battle. I was nearly knocked off my feet with the wave of chaotic and sorrowful energy that hit me when we got there. These days I am more cautious and don't usually open up my spidey senses in places I know have a horrible history. Usually, you get an inkling if you are used to trusting and using your intuition. That feeling you get when you walk into a place, and it feels hinky somehow. Trust your intuition, it won't let you down. Always go into places with your psychic shields at the ready.

I am an animist which means I believe everything has a living energy. Whether it is a pebble from the beach, an herb from the garden, a tree or a 1970s concrete car park. All of these have an energy field. We tap into things such as herbs, plants and crystals to find out what magic they can help us with. We can tap into others such as trees and buildings to make a connection and discover insights, and histories. Tapping into the energy field of the land can bring a strong connection to Mother Nature, spirits of place, deities and ancestors. Do not just take my word for it. Try it.

Exercise: Making a connection

Try this exercise using natural items such as a piece of fruit, a house plant, leaves, feathers and crystals. Use several different items to get a broad range of energies to work with. Also give it a try walking around your garden or your local park. Take a few deep breaths. Rub your hands together for a few seconds. Reach out with both hands either side of the item you are working with. Slowly bring your hands together towards the item. At some point you will hopefully feel a resistance, the edge of the energy field or aura if you prefer the term. Some people feel the energy, others see it, personally I usually feel the energy, but more often than not, I also get words, thoughts or emotions popping into my head.

6
Hedge riding

Let us delve into the Otherworld, leap over the hedge, ride our broomsticks over the boundary and step into other realms. But first I am going to give the bossy, but warranted warnings:

Hedge Riding is the term given for stepping from this world into the other realms and it can be done in various ways. It is important to note this is NOT just meditating, this is going into a deeper trance to cross a boundary. You may enter the unknown, the unfamiliar, the wilds, different places, different times and definitely other realms. You might meet animal spirits, plant spirits, deities or members of the fairy world.

Are there any dangers to hedge riding? Yes, but not if you are sensible. This is not a practice to work with because you are bored or just want to take a relaxing meditation, it does not work like that. This is serious work and requires dedication and experience to work with. I would recommend only attempting hedge riding if you have several years of witchcraft experience behind you. You need to know what you are doing and how to deal with any issues you might come across. This is not an adventure for the novice. Do not hedge ride if you are feeling ill or angry.

I would also advise against hedge riding if you are suffering from any kind of mental illness, it could aggravate your condition and cause you serious mental and emotional harm. Do not go into this unprepared. I usually only hedge ride when I have a reason to do so. Hedge riding can give you insight and guidance into an issue, a problem or help with a decision. But it also has a shamanic side, you can hedge ride to seek out the spirit of a plant or animal to provide healing and wisdom.

Coming out of the hedge riding abruptly or before you have finished can leave you feeling totally spaced out and even quite physically ill. Always ground yourself after any hedge riding, or in fact any energy work at all, otherwise you can be left feeling lightheaded, unfocused or end up with a banging headache.

7
How do you get there?

Whilst some folk like to use hallucinogens, drugs or alcohol to enter a trance state I personally do not advise doing so. There are other methods to use to induce the kind of trance state required that do not endanger your health or safety. You need to allow your subconscious mind to lead the way when you are hedge riding, but you also need your conscious mind to be in control. If they are working together you are safe and also able to see things more clearly.

You do not need any special or magical tools, you are not required to set up an altar or dress in anything particular, unless you want to. Sometimes 'key' items, clothing or paraphernalia can help, it is a personal choice. I don't always cast a circle or perform a ritual, my home is protected anyway and if I am out in nature, the gods look after me, but if you feel drawn to bring in some protection go for it.

Whilst I do not wear anything fancy or specific, you need to feel comfortable, I do work with a blanket that I keep for wrapping around my shoulders specifically when I meditate, journey or hedge ride. Most importantly I use a journey pouch, this is a key item for me.

Rattles and Drums

Rattles and drums can be used to get you into a trance state, but they can also help to clear away any negative energies, call to the spirit guides and help bring in healing energies. I would also advise smudging your room before you begin any journey. I have an amazing stag skin drum that I was honoured and lucky enough to birth myself and it is very special to me. Just the action of beating a simple drum rhythm can work to enter a trance state. But it does not need to be a fancy drum, a tambourine, a rattle or an old cookie tin can be used. You can also source shamanic drumbeats using the music app on your phone.

Ointments

You have probably read or heard about flying ointments, these did actually exist and were usually made from all sorts of nasty and fairly lethal ingredients such as deadly nightshade and foxglove – personally I would avoid these, it's really not worth taking a chance. Instead of an ointment you can use incense blended with herbs and natural items that correspond to contacting the spirit world, otherworld and to aid in psychic abilities. There are some suggestions further on in this book.

Rocking backwards and forwards

This action can help you relax and enter a trance state. Make yourself comfortable in a space where you will not be disturbed. Sitting on the ground is better for this as there is less likelihood of you falling off a chair.

Ground yourself and work with your breath technique. Begin to sway back and forward, keep the rhythm slow and steady. You might also like to include a chant to help. Keep doing this until you find yourself in trance, then you can focus on your purpose. You will often find the swaying movement naturally comes to a stop whilst you are in trance. When you have completed your task, slowly and gently come back to this reality.

Troystones

This method of taking you into trance uses a tool referred to as a 'troystone'. It is a flat piece of wood, ceramic or clay that has a maze or labyrinth carved into the surface. You place the troystone on your lap in front of you and once you have done your grounding and breathwork, you place your finger at the beginning of the carved design. Moving your finger slowly through the maze, spiral or labyrinth pattern it gently takes you into a trance state. This method is helped with the aid of a chant to accompany the journey. It takes a bit of practice and strong concentration to work with a troystone as the images are usually not large and do not take long to move through. It is important to trace the image very slowly and bring in your total attention. Going through the actions too quickly will result in nothing happening.

Journey beads

The idea of journey beads works in a similar way to rosary beads. You hold the string of beads in your hands and slowly pass each bead through your fingers. You can count each bead or use a chant to help enter a trance state.

You could also associate each bead with colours, numbers or words of the chant. I use a set of mala beads.

Chanting

Chanting is a repetitive lyrical way to send yourself off into trance, repeat a phrase or sentence or write yourself a chant to use specifically for hedge riding. You can also play music that helps you enter the otherworld state. Chants can be extremely simple; it is the repetition that helps you enter the trance state. Try using just a few words to begin with, something like 'Hedge ride take me over to see, hedge ride take me over to thee'.

Liminal Spaces

If you are able to physically visit any liminal spaces, you will find the hedge riding experience an interesting one. Sit quietly on the beach at the water's edge or find a comfortable (and safe) spot outside in the countryside beside a hedge then use the landscape as your visual prompt to enter the other worlds. The tree or hedge may already have an obvious portal, but it may also take a bit of searching with your inner eye to find it. Some trees lend themselves to this better than others, I find the older trees usually are excellent, where they are gnarled and twisted.

Hedgerows are also wonderful to work with but be mindful that most of them are on farmland or private property, make sure you have permission to access them. Also be mindful about sitting on a public footpath, you do not want to be disturbed. You do not need to physically jump over the hedge, because that would be difficult and probably quite dangerous. Sit yourself in front of the hedge and spend some time looking at it, really looking, use all your senses and take note of every detail. Then allow yourself to send your spiritual body over the top or through the centre of it.

You can perform the treading the mill or Elder Mother exercise (included within this book) if you prefer or take your stang with you, and use that as the connection between the worlds. I like to keep my eyes open when working with this outside, partly for safety and to be mindful of other folk passing by but also because the natural world also responds to my presence. Keep an open mind and you may see or hear animals or other worldly flickers.

8
State of mind

Let us take a look at what 'going into trance' actually means. To enable you to walk between the worlds you do need to go into another state of mind, this is not the same experience as a regular meditation. The word often used is 'trance' and the dictionary meaning is[1]: 'a half-conscious state characterized by an absence of response to external stimuli, typically as induced by hypnosis or entered by a medium.'

Sometimes you may have a very deep experience but most of the time you will be aware of what is going on about you. You do not lose consciousness; you do not speak in different tongues or host a spirit into your body. For the purpose of hedge riding, you are stepping into another realm but one in which you need to be focused and aware of what is happening. You need to see, hear and sense everything and be able to interact with anything you meet there and ultimately remember it all when you come back to this reality. It takes time, effort and patience to practice, hone and work with this skill properly. This practice is not suitable for everyone one. If you are taking any kind of prescription drugs for mental health issues or recreational drugs of any kind, I would advise you to give this type of practice a miss. You need to be in complete control and focused for this type of work.

---

[1] Oxford dictionary

9
States of Conscious

Let's start by looking at the sciency bit, this involves your states of consciousness, the levels that your mind works on.

When you go into meditation or do any energy work you might notice that your state of consciousness changes. Moving into a different conscious is one of the keys to working with these skills and that includes hedge riding.

If you change your state of consciousness as a voluntary action, then you won't lose yourself. You will be able to still concentrate, still work with energy and still have your intent in place.

This state of conscious was called 'gnosis' by the ancient Greeks, it means 'knowledge'. It is in this state that you can get answers, solve problems, connect with deity and have a psychic connection.

When we go about our daily lives, working, eating, driving etc. our brain waves are in a Beta state. Once we move into meditation or working magic, if we have done it properly our brain waves move into an Alpha state. It is a state of mind where we are relaxed but still aware of what is going on around us. Being in this alpha state (like you are when you are in a daydream) allows you to connect directly with your psychic mind. The next stage is Theta brain waves; this is the level you are at when you enter a deep trance, and the stage you enter when you are asleep. Then you have Delta, which is the level your brain waves are at when you are in a very deep sleep, a very deep trance, or indeed a coma.

10
Our Minds

How many minds do you have? There is the old saying "I am in two minds" but in actual fact we have three. Although some days I am not sure I even have one working mind to be honest. Understanding how our three minds work helps us to work with energy, magic, meditate and gain clarity.

Your conscious mind, your middle self

The mind we are most familiar with is our conscious mind. This is where you will find your personality and your ego. This is the mind that deals with everyday life when we are awake.

The conscious mind houses our reason, our logic, and our ability to analyse and stay alert. It deals with life as a series of events in a timeline, one after another. It sees life as sorted into compartments – past, present and future. The conscious mind is actually pretty good at remembering past events, dealing with the present and working out what it wants for the future, all at the same time. Some days it doesn't seem like it though! It is your conscious mind that works out what you want for yourself and for your magic. It is limited though in that it does see things as linear, which doesn't allow us to work through large amounts of energy or information.

The psychic mind, your lower self, your younger self

The second mind is the psychic mind. This is where you will find the key to your magical abilities. It has no limitations. It works with intuition. Intuition leads us into our psychic abilities.

This mind is called the lower self because it comes from our unconscious and our subconscious. As we relax our logical conscious mind, we move into our subconscious which allows us to see things with greater insight.

Much as it might be a nice idea to always live in your subconscious, we need the balance of the conscious mind and the psychic mind to be able to function properly.

The Divine mind, the higher self, the older self

The psychic mind works as a connection between the conscious mind and the divine mind, which is the third mind or the higher self.

The divine mind is our spirit, it is what connects us to the whole. You can call this mind the Goddess, The God, the Divine Spirit.

This level is a super conscious, a higher self, an older self. It can see things from a higher perspective spiritually and mentally. It is not bound by linear time or logic. It is aware of all things, on all levels, at all times.

The Divine self knows what the conscious mind can handle so it drip feeds information so as not to overwhelm. It is the Divine self that controls our dreams and intuition; it uses the psychic mind to relay this information. These symbols and messages are then deciphered by the unconscious and the subconscious.

The aim is to bring these three minds together so that they work as a team, so they are perfectly aligned. Once you have done this magic, energy work and meditation will be so much easier.

A good little exercise to do each day is to visualise your three selves in harmony. This will have a positive effect on how you feel. Spend a couple of minutes each day, bring the lower self to the middle self, the middle self to the higher self and the higher self to the lower self so that they all harmonise together. When you get used to this exercise you will become aware of any harmony and any conflicts that your three selves have, and you will know where the internal conflicts are.

11
The Three Worlds

We need to take a look at the idea of the three worlds, it is these other worlds that you will step into when you ride the hedge. Each one is unique, and you will find different entities in them. I am going to describe the general ideas, but your experience may be different, there is no definitive here.

The Underworld/Hades/Tir na n-Og/Helheim

The lower world is the one I visit the most often. The Underworld or the Lower World as it is sometimes called is not a deep, dark fiery hell pit, really it isn't. It can however be seen as darker than the middle world. It may often appear as a cave or a very primordial jungle. You can find dangers in the underworld, but you can also meet them in the middle and upper world too. The Underworld is earthy, stable and grounding, it is the base from which the world grows. The Underworld deals with emotions, our intuition and our very basic needs. You may meet ancestors here, animal guides, guardians, plant spirits and the Underworld Kings and Queens along with the fairy realm are found here. If you are very experienced in hedge riding this is also the place to do soul retrieval.

The Middle World/Earth/Midgard/Bith

The middle world is often used as a place for time travel. The middle world is very much like our own and you can find yourself in a place with buildings, houses, cities and the country too. This world is as much full of bad spirits as it is good, so be wary. You will find earth and fertility deities here along with the Elementals, land guardian spirits, messenger deities, nature spirits and the Wild Hunt. I don't visit the middle world regularly; it is mostly used for meeting past and future selves and sometimes the ancestors.

The Upper World/Avalon/Asgard/Olympus

This world is stunning, and I visit here frequently. Spirits live here, and it shows. Think beautiful landscapes, dreamy clouds, sparkling streams and all that is amazing. This is the place to meet and greet spirit guides, Angels, Ascended Masters, Devas, deity and animal guides. It is the upper astral, the spiritual plane and a place of enlightenment. This world will show you knowledge, inspiration, ideas and wisdom and provide healing. The Upper World can also help you remove yourself from your ego and see things as they really are.

12
The Nine Worlds

[1]'I remember yet the giants of yore,
Who gave me bread in the days gone by;
Nine worlds I knew, the nine in the tree
With mighty roots beneath the mold.'

In Norse cosmology the world tree, Yggdrasil is believed to be an ash tree that is host to the nine worlds. These nine worlds are mentioned in the Prose and Poetic Eddas[2]. If you follow a Norse pathway or are drawn to the Norse pantheon it might be worth doing your research and working with these worlds instead of just the three. But please do your homework before you do so, knowledge is power and going in prepared is advisable.

Helheim is the land of the dead and ruled by the goddess Hel, it is the place of human ancestors. Niflheim is a land of ice. Muspelheim is a land of fire. Jotunheim is home to the Jotuns and this is the world where many Norse myths are founded. Svartalfheim is the land of the dwarves. Alfheim is the world of the Alfar, elf home. Vanaheim is home to the Vanir deities. Asgard is home to the Aesir, the main deities in Norse mythology. This land is reached by crossing Bifrost, a rain-

---
1 Voluspo, The Poetic Eddas
2 Pantheon The Norse - Morgan Daimler, 2022

-bow bridge. Midgard is the land of us mere mortal humans. Helheim, Jotunheim and Midgard can be found at the base of the world tree within its roots, the other worlds can be found further up the tree, but exactly where is not clear from any texts.

You can of course work with just three of the Norse worlds – Helheim as the underworld entered through the roots, Midgard as middle earth entered through the trunk in the centre of the tree and Asgard as the upper world and found within the branches. It is your journey, work with it in a way that feels right for you.

13
Breath Work

To really be 'in the zone' I find that breath work is the best place to start. It helps calm and focus your thoughts and takes you on the first step to crossing over the hedge. There are many different types of breathing exercises, experiment and see which works best for you. Be very careful not to overdo any of the breathing exercises, you don't want to end up out of breath or hyperventilating! Here are some suggestions:

Three relaxing breaths

Sit with your mouth closed and your tongue gently resting on your upper palate. Take a slow, deep breath in through your nose, breathe right down into your abdomen, feel it expand and your lungs fill completely. As you breathe in, visualise your mind becoming clear and alert. Hold that breath for a moment. Then exhale slowly through your nose, as you exhale visualise stress flowing out of your body. Hold your lungs empty for a moment. Then repeat again twice.

Bellows Breath

Inhale and exhale rapidly through your nose, keeping your mouth closed (but relaxed). Your breaths in and out should be equal in in duration, but as short as possible, this is a noisy exercise! Aim for three in and out breath cycles per second if you can, it may take practice. Breathe normally after each cycle. Only do this for 10-15 seconds on your first try, each time you try it see if you can last longer, up to a minute in total.

Relaxing

Place the tip of your tongue against the ridge just behind your upper front teeth and keep it there for this entire exercise. Exhale completely through your mouth making a whooshing sound. Close your mouth and inhale quietly through your nose to a count of four (silently in your head). Hold your breath for a count of seven. Exhale completely through your mouth making a whooshing sound for a count of eight. Now inhale again and repeat the cycle three more times.

Once you have worked out which breath work is best for you, begin each session with it. You will not need to focus on your breathing for long, with practice once you start your body will recognise what you are doing, and it will fall into a rhythm it is comfortable with. Then you can move onto the next step.

14
Visualisation

Visualisation is the skill of seeing with your mind's eye. Our mind has the natural ability to create inner landscapes and images. Through creative visualisation we can build these landscapes and step into them to interact with the world we have created. Energy follows our thoughts, so we can use this type of technique in spell-work to visualise our desired outcome and thus make it manifest in reality. It is also through visualisation that we are able to communicate to our subconscious. Our subconscious uses the language of symbols to communicate, we visualise the symbols and are then able to communicate and work magic through it.

For me, good visualisation skills are essential for hedge riding, ritual, spell working and healing of any kind. You do not need to be able to see your visualisations in sharp, clear, high definition, it is not a film show. But you will need to be able to get a picture in your mind of what you want, need, or feel is going on. It might be flashes of images, it could be feelings and emotions along with scents and sounds. Use all your senses to create your visualisations. You can hone your skills by practising visualisation exercises. No, there is short cut to experience, everything worthwhile takes time and effort to achieve.

Exercise: Candle Visualisation

Take a moment to ground and centre yourself and focus on your breathing. Light a candle and look at it. Memorise everything about it, its colour, its height, the holder it is in. Then close your eyes and build the picture of the candle in your mind's eye. If you lose focus and the image starts to fade, open your eyes and look at the candle before closing your eyes again to recreate your candle. Don't worry if your image isn't strong on your first attempt, this is something that can take a bit of practice, but the effort will be worth it.

Once you have mastered the candle visualisation try the next stage: Build the image if the candle again in your mind's eye . Once there, change something about the image. Perhaps the candle colour, add some melting wax dripping down the side, change the holder it is in.

Exercise: Item Visualisation

This works well with a piece of fruit or something edible. Study the item, what colour is it? How does it feel as you hold it in your hand? Is waxy, smooth, cold? Take a bite from it, how does it taste? What scent does it have? Now put the item down. Close your eyes and recreate the image in your mind's eye. Pick your visualised item up. What does it feel like? Take a bite of the visualised item. What does it taste like? Again, this may take some time and you might eat a few things to be able to perfect this exercise.

Once you have worked with, practised and honed your visualisation skills you might like to take a journey into the other world and create a space for yourself. This is a sacred place for just you, a space you can visit whenever you need to. Use it to relax in, to seek guidance or insight in or just a safe space to put your mind into when you feel the need.

15
Shields up!

If you cast a circle or hallow the compass, you have put in place a line of defence against negative energy. But you might like to work in some personal psychic protection as well, I would advise you to do so. This is not a form of protection in case evil entities attach themselves to you once you are on the other side, this just does not happen. Although there are some entities in the other realms that may not be overly friendly or inviting, so it pays to be cautious. Psychic protection will help you to stay focused and to keep your energy levels balanced. There are various methods you can work with, find one that suits you best. The classic is the bubble shield.

Take a few moments to ground and centre yourself. Visualise a giant bubble starting to form around you. The bubble is flexible sphere forming six inches outside your aura. The bubble is completely surrounding you, above your head, down your back, under your feet and in front of you. Your bubble may be clear, or you may want to add some colour to it, the choice is yours. Tell your bubble that it is there to keep anything harmful out, but positive things are able to flow through. When you are ready and no long need your bubble shield, see it gently start to disperse.

Cloak

You may prefer the idea of a cloak: Take a few moments to ground and centre yourself. Visualise putting on a cloak, bring it around your shoulders and close around your neck. Pull the hood up over your head. Feel the cloak moving with you. When you are finished pull back the hood and release the cloak allowing it to fall from your shoulders.

Shield

What about a protective shield as a solider would use in battle? Take a few moments to ground and centre yourself. Put your hand out in front of you and feel a shield form. Feel your hand holding the back of it as the shield fills out, it might be a circle or a rectangle in front of you. It could be made from metal or wood. The shield is now in front of you as protection. When you are finished let go of the shield and allow it to dissipate or fall to the floor.

Crystals

If you like to work with crystals, you can use one as a 'key' to activate your protective shield. It could be a tumble stone you hold in your hand or a piece of jewellery such as a pendant you tap to activate. Visualise a field of energy emanating from the crystal and providing you with a protective shield. Once you are finished, tap the crystal again and allow the shield to be pulled back into the stone.

16
Grounding

One technique that I believe is incredibly important to work with after any kind of energy work, particularly when you have been on a journey is grounding. It is really simple to do but incredibly effective. Not grounding your energies can leave you feeling lightheaded, fuzzy, bleary and can give you a cracking headache.

Methods of grounding: Perhaps the most recognised method is to visualise yourself as a tree. Begin by closing your eyes and focusing on your breathing, deep breaths in and deep breaths out. Now see roots coming out from the soles of your feet, stretching down through the earth into the soil beneath. Send your roots right down and allow any excess energy to flow out through them. Once you feel that you are balanced you can slowly begin to draw your roots back up again. Clapping your hands and stamping your feet can help release any excess energy. Placing the palms of your hands face down on the ground, allowing any excess energy to flow into the soil. Hold onto a pebble or stone and allow it to absorb any excess energy. Eat and drink something, chocolate is particularly good for this.

17
Chants

Whether you choose to use them when entering the Otherworld, to raise energy or for spell work, chants and rhymes can be incredibly useful. You can make your own obviously, and I can highly recommend using one of the online rhyming dictionaries to assist you. I like to look at ancient charms and folk chants for inspiration or use as they are, some of them are fascinating. Here are a selection and their suggested uses: ¹Ode to the Trees from the Buile Suibhne. This works well to recite before you cross the hedge, it calls upon the spirits of many beautiful trees and a lot that are found in the hedgerows.

Thou oak, bushy, leafy,
thou art high beyond trees;
O hazlet, little branching one,
O fragrance of hazel-nuts.

O alder, thou art not hostile,
delightful is thy hue,
thou art not rending and prickling
in the gap wherein thou art.

---

1   A medieval Irish tale

O little blackthorn, little thorny one;
O little black sloe-tree;
O watercress, little green-topped one,
from the brink of the ousel(?) spring.

O minen of the pathway,
thou art sweet beyond herbs,
O little green one, very green one,
O herb on which grows the strawberry.

O apple-tree, little apple-tree,
much art thou shaken;
O quicken, little berried one,
delightful is thy bloom.

O briar, little arched one,
thou grantest no fair terms,
thou ceasest not to tear me,
till thou hast thy fill of blood.

O yew-tree, little yew-tree,
in churchyards thou art conspicuous;
o ivy, little ivy,

thou art familiar in the dusky wood.

O holly, little sheltering one,
thou door against the wind;
o ash-tree, thou baleful one,
hand-weapon of a warrior.

O birch, smooth and blessed,
thou melodious, proud one,
delightful each entwining branch
in the top of thy crown.

The aspen a-trembling;
by turns I hear
its leaves a-racing—
meseems 'tis the foray!

Calling to the sea winds from Otia Merseiana II[1]. This can be used quite successfully if you are in the liminal space at the edge of the ocean.

When the wind sets from the east,
the spirit of the wave is roused,
So that it desires to go past us westward
to the land where sets the sun
To the rough and broad green sea.
When the wind sets from the north,
it urges the dark fierce waves
Towards the southern world,

surging in strife against the white sky,
Listening to the song.

When the wind sets from the west
across the salt sea of swift currents,

---

[1] Song of the sea, ascribed to Ruman mac Colmáin from Irish manuscripts 4 in Otia Merseiana

It desires to go past us eastward
to the sun-tree
Into the broad long distant sea.
When the wind sets from the south
across the land of Saxons of mighty shields

A protection charm[1]

This can be used for physical, psychic or spiritual protection. A charme to be said each morning by a witch fasting, or at least before she go abroad. THE fier bites, the fier bites, the fier bites; Hogs turd over it, hogs turd over it, hogs turd over it; The father with thee, the sonne with me, the holie-ghost betweene us both to be: Then spit over one shoulder, and then over the other, and then three times right forward.

House protection charm

A charme to drive awaie spirits that haunt anie house. HAng in everie of the foure corners of your house this sentence written upon virgine parchment; Omnis spiritus laudet Dominum: Mosen habent & prophetas: Exurgat Deus et dissi/pentur inimici ejus.

Herb gathering charm

This can be said as you collect your herbs, if you are uncomfortable with using the name Jesus you could substitute it with something else perhaps 'Mother Earth' or the 'Goddess. Another charme that witches use at the gathering of their medicinable hearbs.

---

1   A Discoverie of Witchcraft, Reginald Scott, 1584

Haile be thou holie hearbe
growing on the ground
All in the mount *Calvarie* Though neither the hearbe nor the witch never came there.
first wert thou found,
Thou art good for manie a sore,
And healest manie a wound,
In the name of sweete Jesus
I take thee from the ground.

Yggdrasil

This is part of the poetic Eddas which works nicely to begin your Otherworld journey if you wish to venture into the nine worlds. The three maidens named refer to the Norns, the goddesses of fate, past, present and future.

[1]An ash I know, Yggdrasil its name,
With water white is the great tree wet;
Thence come the dews that fall in the dales,
Green by Urth's well does it ever grow.

Thence come the maidens mighty in wisdom,
Three from the dwelling down 'neath the tree;
Urth is one named, Verthandi the next,--
On the wood they scored, and Skuld the third.
Laws they made there, and life allotted
To the sons of men, and set their fates.

---

[1] Voluspo, Poetic Eddas

Witch flight charm

This is an old folk chant that can be used to begin your hedge riding journey, I recommend repeating it as a rhythmic chant.

Stone invocation

This little invocation gives thanks for finding a pebble or stone but could be used for anything such as a feather or plant.

[1]'I have found
A holy-stone upon the ground.
O Fate! I thank thee for the happy find,
Also the spirit who upon this road
Hath given it to me;
And may it prove to be for my true good
And my good fortune!

---

1   Aradia: Gospel of the Witches, Charls Godfrey Leland, 1899

18
Smudging

Before you begin a hedge riding journey I would advise smudging the room you will be in, if indoors and your body. This makes sure your setting and physical body are clear of any negative energy. Cleansing an area with smoke is ancient and the method has been used by many cultures, for good reason, because it works. However, if you are unable to use smoke I would recommend creating a loose incense blend of herbs and resins and popping it in the top of an oil burner. The heat from the candle warms the herbals and sends out a scent but without the smoke. If you are not able to use any kind of scent, then salt is a good alternative, sprinkle it into the corners of the room or area. If you prefer you can make a room and body mist instead.

You can make your own herb bundles by tying together stalks of herbs, wrap them firmly with twine (make sure it is natural as you will be burning it) and allow them to dry. You might need to adjust the twine once the herbs are fully dried as they tend to shrink a little. If you prefer you can put together a loose incense mixture and use that instead. You can use all sorts of herbs and florals, my suggestions are below, these have been selected as they all carry the property of cleansing and purification. These also work well in herb bundles as the herbs have long stalks, or if from a tree then twigs can be used. Soft herbs and flower petals can be used but I would wrap them around the outside of the bundle as they will burn quickly. Agrimony, alexanders, bay, birch, cedar, elder, eucalyptus, geranium, hawthorn, heather, juniper, lavender, mint, mugwort, pine, rosemary, sage, sweetgrass, tansy, thyme, valerian, vervain.

If you are creating a cleansing and purifying incense blend to use rather than an herb bundle, you could add in: Frankincense, copal, fennel seeds, juniper berries, star anise or myrrh.

Begin by making some physical space, light your herb bundle or incense and begin at one side/edge of the room or area. I like to walk round in an anti-clockwise direction. Waft the smoke or scent away from you and into the area you want to cleanse and purify. Walk slowly and make sure the smoke gets into the corners. Complete a full circuit of the area. As you walk visualise the smoke cleansing and clearing away any negative energy, if you like you can add in a chant, something like:

Herbal smoke to cleanse and clear
Purify this area so there is no fear
Remove negativity and make it safe for me
Bring in protection and positivity

Don't forget to cleanse and purify your physical body too. If you have the space, you can place the herb bundle or incense safely on the floor and step over it and through the smoke. Using an herb bundle you can also pass it around your body, along your arms and legs, up over your head, front and back and under your feet.

On occasion when I have been caught out and about and in the need of cleansing and purifying, I have used a packet of peppermint sweets!

Room and Body Mist

These are easy to make, and you can add different oils and herbs to suit your intent. Basic recipe:

180ml/6 fl oz distilled water
24 drops essential oil
Petals, herb leaves or spices

To make a hedge riding mist I would recommend oils such as pine, lavender, mint, rosemary, frankincense, geranium and cedar. Experiment and see which blends work well for you. Note: Distilled water can be created by boiling water in a kettle and allowing it to cool.

19
The Spoken Word

Charms involve the spoken word to work magic. This can be in the form of speaking words direct from your heart or working it into a chant or rhyme. This is the part of your spell where you put your request into words. If you are poetic then chants and rhymes work really well, they are quite musical and can give your spell working a good flow. My poetic skills are rubbish, so I do rely on a rhyming dictionary from the internet, these are a total blessing and really help when crafting a chant.

However, if you prefer you can just speak the words, clearly and concisely, it must work for you. Say it in your head, whisper it or say it out loud, doesn't matter, do what works for you. Say it once, say it three times, bring in number magic, do what works for you. Most importantly be clear about your goal, your intent, who, what, where and when.

20
Offerings

It makes sense and I believe it is also good manners to give offerings when you undertake any kind of work that involves connection with the Otherworld. Sometimes I make an offering on my altar or outside before a journey but mostly I make an offering afterwards. This works because I then know who I met and what an appropriate offering would be. There are no right or wrong items to give as offerings, trust your intuition. Sometimes whoever you meet in your journey will ask for something specific. It might be in the form of a food or drink offering, it could be herbs or crystals set out on your altar or it might be feeding the birds. Offerings can be set out on your altar; I have a small offering dish set up for that purpose. If I am using food or drink I only leave it out for a day, then I throw it out into the garden. Crystals get cleansed and stored away for use again.

21
Staff, Stang and Besom

If you like to work with a physical item to help you step into the other world a staff, stang or besom work well. They can be used as representations of the world tree. A staff or stang is also useful when out walking and foraging for poking about in the undergrowth and pulling down overhanging tree branches to reach the fruit or seeds. Practical and spiritual.

A stang is a wooden staff with two prongs, these represent the meeting of two worlds, two energies, the masculine and the feminine. I have used both a stang and a carved wooden staff, with equal success. You can use just a fallen stick that you find when out and about. A besom works as well but can be a bit cumbersome. If you prefer you can also work with a wand, it is after all perhaps just a miniature staff?

If you are looking at getting a staff, stang or wand do have a look into the magical properties of the wood they are made from, this can be useful when seeking one specifically for hedge riding. A staff or wand can be made from a fallen branch or stick, you can put out a request when you go for a walk and see what nature provides for you. It can be kept as is, with the bark still on, eau naturel so to speak. Or you can strip the bark, sand the wood and oil or varnish it.

Symbols or sigils can be carved into the wood if you feel drawn to do so. Feathers, beads and crystals can be attached to the top as well. It really is personal choice, but I find it good to go with what the wood instructs me to do.

I am very lucky to have been gifted several staffs. My stang is very plain and simple, just dark wood with nothing fancy on it or attached to it. One staff is heavy solid oak, has my name and oak leaves cared down the length and has been stripped, sanded and varnished. The other staff is light ash wood, stripped and oiled with a beautiful horse head carving on the top, I have tied beads and a black obsidian arrow point to the top. All three have been used for hedge riding and all work brilliantly, I use whichever one I am drawn to on the day.

[1]The term 'stang' derives from Old Norse, 'stong' or 'stange' and means 'pole'. Sometimes you will find a stang that has been created using horns or antlers on the top and often a traditional stang will include an iron nail at the base, reminiscent of a horseshoe. This idea suggests the representation of a horse for the magical practitioner to ride over into the other realms.

The stang provides several uses for magical purpose. One of those is to create the hallowing of the compass and another is to serve as a portable altar. Your stang can also be used like a wand, to direct energy. For the purpose of hedge riding the stang becomes a representation of the world tree, the [2]axis mundi and is used as the centre point for your journey.

---
1   Treading the Mill, Nigel Pearson, 2017
2   : world axis: line or stem through the earth's center connecting

Whilst a stang is occasionally used in ritual to represent both the goddess and the god, it really is the Old One, the Horned One, the Horned God. The besom or broom has a wooden handle with twigs fastened at one end. It can be used for the practical purpose of sweeping floors, but also is used in ritual to symbolically sweep away negative energy when preparing for ritual.

The besom is a symbol of flying over the hedge or crossing into the Otherworld. This means the besom too can be used for hedge riding in a similar way to the stang. A traditional besom is often made from three types of wood; the handle from ash, the brushes from birch twigs which are bound with willow. A traditional besom is never fixed with wire or metal. The besom balances nicely with the stang as it carries strong feminine energies to counter the stang's masculine. You will be familiar with the besom at handfasting's where the couple jump the broomstick, this represents crossing over from one state (the single life) to another (being a couple).

---

its surface to the underworld and the heavens and around which the universe revolves – Merriam Webster dictionary.

22
Journey Bag

Many hedge witches (and shamanic practitioners) have a 'journey bag' they use to keep magical items in to aid in their travels to the Otherworld. Every bag will be personal and specific to each individual, it might contain beads, shells, feathers, pebbles, herbs and crystals – if you decide to make your own bag be guided by your intuition and add whatever you feel is necessary to help you on your hedge riding.

I purchased a 'fat quarter' piece of fabric (approx. 50x55cm or 19x22") from a haberdashery. Fat quarters are an excellent way of purchasing smaller pieces of fabric at a reasonable price that can be used as altar clothes, to wrap tarot or oracle cards or to create journey bags. If you look in the autumn, you can often find spooky/witchy themed fat quarters too. My piece of fabric is folded up with the items inside and then tied with a piece of leather thong and it sits on my altar.

When I am ready to journey, I undo the bag and open the fabric out flat to show the contents. Inside I have all sorts of things and they change from time to time depending on how I feel or what I feel it needs added or taken away. There are crystals and herbs that are associated with psychic abilities, astral travel and the Otherworld.

Also included is a brooch that belonged to my grandmother and an RAF badge that belonged to my great uncle, both who have now passed.

Then I have some random items such as a brooch depicting Arthur and the sword in the stone as I associate this with Avalon. There is a silver sixpence as silver is a magical metal. A small ceramic dragon as I work with dragon magic, and it provides me protection on my journeys. A small pentacle to represent the elements and their qualities. A feather to help my intuition and a charm to represent my animal spirit guide. I also have a piece of sea glass to help balance my emotions, a hag stone for wisdom and a button to open the doorways.

Herbs suggestions

These are all associated with the magic of psychic abilities, astral travel or the Otherworld. These can be used in journey bags, incense blends, spell work or to dress candles: Almond, apple, bay, borage, buttercup, cinnamon, cornflower, dandelion, grass, heather, honeysuckle, juniper, mace, marigold, mugwort, mustard, parsley, rose, rowan, saffron, sage, sea holly, star anise, tansy, thistle, thyme, tobacco, valerian, wormwood, yarrow, yew.

Crystal suggestions

These are all associated with the magic of psychic abilities, astral travel or the Otherworld. These can be used in journey bags, incense blends, spell work or held in your hand on your journey: Amber, green aventurine, celestite, chrysocolla, Citrine, copper, garnet, howlite, kyanite, labradorite, lepidolite, malachite, moonstone, black obsidian, pyrite, clear quartz, rhodonite, selenite, silver, sodalite, sugilite, tiger's eye, tourmaline, turquoise.

Other items you could add to your journey bag: Items to represent the elements of earth, air, fire and water such as a pebble, a feather, a matchstick and a shell. Buttons to open and close doorways. Pictures of your ancestors or items that belonged to them. Images of your spirit animal guide. Small animal bones or teeth, these can help link you to the Otherworld and your spirit animal guide. Be guided by your intuition and what you feel needs to be added. Remember the contents of your journey bag or not static they can be removed or added to at any time.

23
Spirits of all kinds

One of the areas you will work with as a Hedge Witch is spirits, and these come in many forms. Note that I am not talking about what a psychic medium does, this is not table tipping, knocking on the table three times or asking, 'is there anyone there'. What a medium does is different, although just to complicate things, some Hedge Witches do work with mediumship too (as I do), but it is an area that requires training and specifics that are not related to hedge riding. Here I give an explanation of the spirits that we do work with when we jump the hedge to the Otherworld.

This is all part of what is called [1]animism. Animism means that we believe all things have an energy field, an aura if you prefer to use that term. It does not matter if it is a pebble, a leaf, a crystal or a tree, these all have an energy that we can connect with. That connection taps us into the spirit of the item and can guide us, in the case of herbs and crystals the spirit can show us what magic they can help us with. For plants and trees, the spirit connection can help us with wisdom, insight and healing. For example, when a hedge witch journeys into the other world to connect with a plant spirit it is often to seek healing or help with a spell.

---

1   the belief that all natural things, such as plants, animals, rocks, and thunder, have spirits and can influence human events – Cambridge dictionary.

Do remember that spirits in the Otherworld may not have the same idea about morals or etiquette as we do. They may not act or react in a way we would expect them to, nor should they, they have no need to follow our rules.

There are no hard and fast categories either, some entities straggle two or more and others do not fall into any specific category. Some entities may be called a specific name in one country and something else in another. Trying to identify, label and categorise them all would be a logistical nightmare and actually quite rude to be honest. They do not fall into our way of thinking, and neither should they. Be open to whatever or whoever you meet, be mindful of respecting them at all times but also be wary.

You may find what I call 'spirits of place' these are often nature spirits for want of a better term. They are the energies of a location, sometimes fae, often spirits of trees and plants and sometimes ancestors or echoes of those that have lived on the land before. These are sometimes referred to as 'land wights'. These spirits can be very protective of their area or specific trees and plants. They act as guardians of the area and are very good at shapeshifting. Your home will also have a spirit energy of some kind, again I am not referring to ghosts wandering through your kitchen, but the energy that your house holds within the walls and beneath the floors.

Animal spirits are another form of spirit energy you may encounter on your journeys. This is a particular favourite of mine as the spirit animal can provide us with so much in the form of support, wisdom and insight. Be open to whatever animal you discover, treat it with respect and pay attention to any wisdom it has to impart to you.

[1]Fetch – this one is a bit more complicated. Fetch is an Irish folklore term that means a spirit guide which can be in the form of a person or an animal. There are varying beliefs about the fetch some say that it is the true spirit of a person and appears in three forms; the fetch beast, which equates to our ideas of a spirit animal guide, the fetch wyf, a contra sexual spirit of the person whom it guides and the fetch god which is the divine face of our own fetch.

Fetch can also mean a spirit doppelganger spirit that takes on the appearance of someone who has just died or is about to die. It is not actually the ghost of a person but an imitation of someone who is still alive. Although folklore states that seeing a fetch is a sign that the person it portrays is about to die.

Similarly, the word fylgja is from the Norse tradition and means the same as a fetch - a spirit (person or animal) who accompanies a person in connection to their fate or fortune. A Norse vitki (sorcerer) would not only draw power from his fylgia but could also project his conscious will into it in order for it to carry out magical workings. The fylgia brought huge responsibilities and power but could also throw hardships and challenges into the mix too. The fylgia would mould itself to the personality of the person it was attached to, and the well-being of the human would depend on the well-being of the animal fylgia. Many Norse believed that the fylgia was in fact part of the hugr or soul and that it was capable of leaving the body and projecting itself elsewhere.

At some point when travelling into the Otherworld you may

---

[1] Pagan Portals Animal Magic, Rachel Patterson

find you connect with ancestors in some form. These are not necessarily ghosts of your loved ones in the sense that a medium would connect with them in. They are in the form of echoes or imprints of ancestors left behind that become part of the land we live on. They may still retain a faint representation of their old selves, something that we might recognise in some way, but they have essentially become spirits of the land.

Wherever you are the land beneath your feet will hold memories of those that have lived or worked there before. The land also holds onto events and happenings particularly if they were dramatic in some way. Be mindful that not all of these ancestors or memories of events are good ones, sometimes they can be overwhelming. Be prepared to disconnect or retreat from the energy if you feel uncomfortable, remember you are always in control.

24
The Fair Folk

Then we have the Fair Folk, the Elven kind or the world of Fairy. What I am also not going to do is write lots about the fair folk. You may well encounter beings from the fairy world when you hedge ride or even when you are out and about. Once you have opened up that portal to the Otherworld they do sometimes overlap into the mundane world.

However, I firmly believe that working with the world of fairy is a calling, a dedication and a serious commitment. The fair folk are not to be dabbled with or seen as fluffy, delightful creatures in stripy tights and tutus. All you need to do is look at old fairy tales and fae legend to discover how dark the world of fairy can be. There is also a very strict etiquette for dealing with the fair folk. I am not discouraging you from building a relationship with them, if you do, it can be very rewarding. But I do advise caution and that you take a lot of time and effort into researching the best ways of working with them. There are a lot of pitfalls to be avoided and lessons that need taking on board before you begin your journey with them. Always treat them with respect and good manners although this is an area that needs a lot of research, for instance, saying 'thank you' to a fairy means nothing to them. They do like offerings and gifts but be wary that they do not see it as a bargain or an exchange for something you might not want to commit to. Respect nature, it is there home, but then you should do that anyway without question.

There is a long-held belief that you should not eat or drink anything offered to you by the fae, there are different situations for this and definite guidelines, do your research. Time in the world of fairy runs at a different pace, be mindful of this.

25
The Gods

I am not going to discuss at any great length, the gods and goddesses. Whilst they do appear in a lot of witchcraft books (a lot of my own include them), you don't need to work with or even believe in deity or the divine to be a Hedge Witch. Nature provides its own magic and divine energy, whether you see that as the Goddess, Gaia, the Horned God, the Green Man, Mother Earth, Father Sky or just the spirit of each natural place is up to you.

What I would recommend you do is some local research. Each culture has its own pantheon of deities, but also folk lore and legends often attached to each location. For me in England our myths and legends relating to gods is very sparse, in fact almost non-existent. We do have ancient deities; it is just that a lot of them have been forgotten. Some of them were highlighted and kept 'alive' when the Romans were here, piggy backed with some of their chosen gods, but most were buried under layers of history. Ancient Britons did not write anything down, all that we have are odd mentions in Roman history or a few archaeological items. What we do know is that most of the ancient English deities were tied to one place, often a river and usually began life as a spirit of the place. My personal mission is to seek these old gods out and shine a light on them again, it may take me some time.

But by getting to know the legends and myths in your own area is another way of making a connection. You may also find that some of these divine beings appear when you are hedge riding.

If you want to work with deity, do your research. Working with deity is a relationship, just like any other relationship you have so it takes time, effort and commitment. Learn about them, their stories, myths and legends, where they come from, their culture, homeland and even what foods and plants grow there.

Take time to build a relationship with them, find out their likes and dislikes and each of their individual personalities.

Working with deity is very rewarding, they can provide you with support, insight, guidance and assistance with your magic. They can also reprimand you, judge you and kick your butt, I speak from experience here when I say they do exactly that, but they are always right in doing so. I do not like to use the word 'worship' because I don't see my relationship with deity as that, I work with them, and they walk beside me. But you do not need a connection or belief in them to be able to successfully hedge ride.

26
Preparation

Hedge riding is more than meditation, much more, it is similar to pathworking, sometimes called journeying, inner plane work or vision quests. It is a structured form of meditation with a purpose to it, a guided journey into the Otherworld and it goes much deeper than regular meditation. Hedge riding journeys need some preparation.

Once you are experienced you may not need to lay out every little detail each time, but if you are a beginner, it really helps to have that framework in place. Start with the setting, are you going to include your hedge ride within a full ritual or hallowing the compass, or just a stand-alone journey? Then the induction, how are you going to put yourself into a trance like state? Will you tread the mill, drum or something else?

Plan out your journey beginning with the image you will use to step over the hedge, or through the tree. Decide what you need from this trip, why are you journeying? What portal will you take? What is your destination? What or who would you like to encounter? Obviously, you will probably encounter some things you didn't plan for but that makes it even more worthwhile. Will you set out specific can-

where will you set it down, and does it need any additions?

I find it also pays to take a moment to fix the entry place in your mind once you have stepped through. Reach out to touch the entry way, how does it feel, smell or any sounds. This just helps you find your way back to the entry point once you are finished with your hedge ride journey.

If your hedge ride is to meet a specific animal or plant spirit, do some research, make sure you know what it looks like, where it grows or lives and what habit you should be looking for. Being prepared makes for a more successful and productive hedge ride.

27
Ritual

Lots of spiritual folk will perform a full ritual when working any kind of magic or journey. I do not. When working within my own home my boundaries are regularly protected so I don't feel the need to bring in extra protection when I hedge ride or indeed when I work any kind of spell.

You may feel more comfortable bringing in a full ritual structure around your hedge riding. The basic structure that you are probably familiar with reflects a Wiccan ritual, so I have given the outline for you to adapt to your own liking. When I work with a ritual structure for hedge riding I tend to use the Hallowing the Compass route, which is included below as well. Use all of the ritual structure, just parts of it or none at all, the choice is yours.

Hallowing the compass

The idea of a compass uses the basis of a circle similar to casting the circle, an idea we are probably all more familiar with. However here the circle casting and quarter calling are combined to use the idea of a compass as the protective circle, the boundary between the worlds, creating your own liminal space. It could be called conjuring the circle, laying the round, ploughing the furrow or simply creating sacred space.

You can make it as grand or as simple as you like, but for the solitary practitioner I like to keep it straightforward, and it can just literally be walking around the edge of your sacred space to create a circle. The idea is to create a space that is separate from the mundane world, and area that is designated as sacred and magical, one that you can step into to perform magic and/or connect with the Otherworld in. It can also be used to provide a circle of protection. Once you have set your compass area it becomes sacred and just outside of the usual restrictions of the mundane world. What you create basically is a portal to the Otherworld or if you want to think about it like this, hallowing the compass creates a magical hedge, a boundary between the worlds that we may step over, or in fact, hedge ride.

What do you need to hallow the compass? Nothing physical, but what you do need is your energy and visualisation skills. You have to create the boundary using your own intent. You can walk around the area, you can chant or say magical words, but if you don't lend your intent, will and energy to create it then all you are doing is walking and talking. The portal will only be created if you make it happen, it takes work and effort. Some will 'see' the compass as a flat circle, others prefer to expand that circle and create a sphere going above and below, do what works for you, there is no right or wrong here.

My chant for hallowing the compass circle:
As I walk a compass circle I create around
To my sacred space I am bound
Energy created stays within
Protection now as I begin

Once your compass circle has been put in place you can fix it in or give it a more physical presence by calling in the elements from each of the compass directions. What you are doing is inviting the spiritual energy from each of the compass directions to lend their magic to your ritual or working. This is not essential to do and you can just work with the compass circle as it is, but this does lend another layer of energy to whatever you are working with. The four elements of earth, air, fire and water are actually already with us in all that we do but inviting them in helps you become more aware of them and their characteristics and makes it easier for you to work with them. I work with the elements at these compass points:

                Earth – North
                Air – East
                Fire – South
                Water – West

There is no right or wrong here, work with them as you feel is right. It may also depend on where in the world you are, what part of the country you are in or what the natural landscape is around you. I have a lovely old-fashioned brass compass but have also used a compass app on my phone. If you are familiar with watching the sun and where it rises and sets that can also be used. Having said that, I have also worked with the lay of the landscape rather than the cardinal points of the compass. When I have been working on the seashore I used the ocean as west, if I am working near a bonfire or on a particularly hot summer's day I use that direction as south. But it has to feel right for you. Trust your intuition on this one. You are creating and forming pathways within your circle compass that lead to and from the centre.

It is also important to note that when you invite the elements or deity into your compass circle or to join you in ritual, they do not have to acquiesce to your request. It is also worth bearing in mind that all the elements and even deity to some extent are ever present, even if you 'dismiss' them from your rite, they will still be there. When you invite them to join you, you are asking them to lend their energies, wisdom, support and presence to your ritual and whatever spell work or journeying you are working with. It is only right and proper to thank them for their help and assistance once you are done. They will not disappear completely because they are always around, but you have let them know that you no longer require their immediate attention.

If you have a stang or staff, use it to mark each compass point. Start with north and place your staff upright in the ground at the north point of your compass circle. Walk back to the centre of the compass circle and face your staff. See and feel the energy of that element. Then walk to your staff, take it in your hand and use it to 'draw' the circle from the north point to the next compass point, see the circle being formed as you draw the curve of the line. Place your staff upright in the ground at the next compass point and repeat your actions by walking to the centre and facing the direction, seeing and feeling the element energy coming in. Repeat this until you have brought together all four compass points and drawn your compass circle. You can say a chant as you do this or just work with your visualisations. You can walk the circle once or I like to do this three times, sometimes it takes a few more circuits, it depends on the situation.

The idea of walking the edge of the compass is to create that sacred place inside and to separate you from the real world. You should feel a change in the atmosphere. If you don't have a staff or stang you can do this using your wand or just your finger.

My chant suggestions:

As I stand inside the compass facing north
I invite the element of earth to come forth
Mountains, rocks and valleys deep
The stability and grounding of earth to meet

As I stand inside the compass facing east
I invite the element of air to sweep
Fresh breeze and wind blow in
Bringing intellect and inspiration with

As I stand inside the compass facing south
I invite the element of fire to flame
Bonfire, heat and solar rays
Bringing transformation and passion says

As I stand inside the compass facing west
I invite the element of water to rest
Streams and rivers flowing free
Bringing the balance of emotions to me

Once you have done this return to the centre. Notice how the inside of the compass circle feels. If you like you can also visualise the circle extending to cover above and below you, forming a sphere. Then connect with the four compass directions, feel the energy from each of the elements connecting with you.

Once you have hallowed the compass you have opened a sacred space that gives you access to the Otherworld, so it is only right and sensible to close it down once you have finished with it.

This is a very simple process. Begin by standing in the centre of the sacred space and allow the elements to release, let the lines of the sphere retract back from the centre to the outer edges. I like to use these chants alongside visualisation.

As I stand inside the compass facing west
I release the element of water now it rests

As I stand inside the compass facing south
I release the element of fire and flame

As I stand inside the compass facing east
I release the element of air not least

As I stand inside the compass facing north
I release the element of earth and force

Walk in the opposite direction around the perimeter allowing the circle to dissipate. Let the energy flow back into Mother Earth or up into Father Sky. You can sweep the circle if you prefer, clearing away the energy of the compass.

As I release the compass circle I say:

As I walk the compass circle I created
My circle ring is now deflated
Energy released to do some good
Protection stays with me as it should

Now ground yourself! This is really important after any kind of energy work. Clap your hands, stamp your feet or place your hands palms down onto the earth and allow any excess energy to drain out. Eating and drinking something also helps, any excuse for cake or chocolate is good with me.

Thank the deity or any divine beings you have worked with. I like to give an offering at this point as a way of thanks. Pouring a libation or crumbling some food onto the earth works well. If you prefer here is an outline for a basic Wiccan ritual structure: Cast your circle by walking or turning clockwise (dependent on the space you are in) As you walk visualise a circle or protection forming around you and then above and below you. Saying a chant can help, such as:

Hedge of nature, wild and free
Bring in a circle of protection for me

Then call in the quarters, inviting the elements in from each compass direction, visualise their energy joining you in your circle.

Facing north, say: Element of earth I invite you to bring stability and grounding to my rite, welcome.

Facing east, say: Element of air I invite you to bring intellect and intuition to my rite, welcome.

Facing west, say: Element of water I invite you to bring your strength of emotion to my rite, welcome.

Facing south, say: Element of fire I invite you to bring passion and transformation to my rite, welcome.

Then work with your preferred method of hedge riding. Once you are finished you will need to close down the ritual structure. Thank each of the elements in turn in reverse order, just a simple 'thank you for lending your energy to my rite' is fine. Then take down your circle by walking or turning anti clockwise and visualising the sphere dissipating. Saying: Hedge of nature, with thanks from me, I release your protection and set the energy free.

It can take time to connect with the directions and the elements that represent them. I have given my preferences here and the characteristics that I associate with them. You may find it different. This is about building a relationship and making connections, get to know them. My suggestion is to journey to meet them and find out what they mean to you. Once you have done this and built a relationship then you can all upon them in ritual to assist you. You might like to split this into four separate journeys or work with it as a whole, do what works for you.

Journey to meet the Elements

Make yourself comfortable somewhere you will not be disturbed. You can read through this text and commit the journey outline to memory, or you can record it and play it back as a guided journey. Have a notebook handy to jot down information afterwards. Focus on your breathing, deep breaths in and deep breaths out.

As your world around you dissipates you find yourself walking along a dusty country trackway. On one side there are tall trees marking the edge of a woodland and on the other side is a hedgerow with a steep grassy bank behind it.

Look at the landscape surrounding you as you walk, open all your senses, looking and listening with each step you take. The track way leads you to a crossroads and once you reach the centre you stop. Take a good look around you in each direction. At the centre of the crossroads is an old wooden signpost, on each side of the sign is a different direction; north, east, south and west.

Turn to the direction marked north and begin walking along the track. Part way down the track the air in front of you begins to shimmer and the landscape behind it appears blurry. It seems to form a portal, do not feel afraid. Step forward and through the shimmery area. This is north on the compass, what do you see once you are through the portal? Ask for the powers of the north to make themselves known. You may hear words, feel sensations or emotions and you may meet a being, guardian or spirit. Be open to whatever comes to you and ask questions about the power they represent. Once you are finished, give your thanks if you met anyone and turn, stepping back through the portal and once more onto the dusty road. Turn and head back to the centre of the crossroads.

Once back at the centre, turn and walk in the direction marked east. Part way down the track the air in front of you begins to shimmer and the landscape behind it appears blurry. It seems to form a portal, do not feel afraid. Step forward and through the shimmery area. This is east on the compass, what do you see once you are through the portal? Ask for the powers of the east to make themselves known. You may hear words, feel sensations or emotions and you may meet a being, guardian or spirit. Be open to whatever comes to you and ask questions about the power they represent. Once you are finished, give your thanks if you met anyone and turn, stepping back through the portal and once more onto the dusty road. Turn and head back to the centre of the crossroads.

Once back at the centre, turn and walk in the direction marked south. Part way down the track the air in front of you begins to shimmer and the landscape behind it appears blurry. It seems to form a portal, do not feel afraid. Step forward and through the shimmery area. This is south on the compass, what do you see once you are through the portal? Ask for the powers of the south to make themselves known. You may hear words, feel sensations or emotions and you may meet a being, guardian or spirit. Be open to whatever comes to you and ask questions about the power they represent. Once you are finished, give your thanks if you met anyone and turn, stepping back through the portal and once more onto the dusty road. Turn and head back to the centre of the crossroads.

Once back at the centre, turn and talk in the direction marked west. Part way down the track the air in front of you begins to shimmer and the landscape behind it appears blurry. It seems to form a portal, do not feel afraid. Step forward and through the shimmery area. This is west on the compass, what do you see once you are through the portal? Ask for the powers of the west to make themselves known. You may hear words, feel sensations or emotions and you may meet a being, guardian or spirit. Be open to whatever comes to you and ask questions about the power they represent. Once you are finished, give your thanks if you met anyone and turn, stepping back through the portal and once more onto the dusty road. Turn and head back to the centre of the crossroads.

Once back at the centre, focus once again on your breathing. And slowly and gently come back to the here and now.

Open your eyes and wriggle your fingers and toes. Jot down any important points. Know that this place is here for you to visit whenever you feel the need and to connect in more detail with the elements. Bear in mind it may take some time to get a real connection and also to discover what characteristics and energies each direction represents and can bring into your life.

Treading the Mill

Treading, pacing or working the Mill is a technique used in Traditional Witchcraft and it does what it says on the tin. You have a fixed point in the centre, usually a stang or a staff and you tread around it in a circle. Think about the idea of a donkey walking around and around turning a millstone to grind the wheat and you have the right idea. Not that I am suggestion you are a donkey obviously! The physical movement of walking in a circle whilst keeping your eyes focused on the central point helps to put you in the state of mind you need to ride the hedge.

However, it can also be used to raise energy if you need to for the purpose of spell casting. This practice can be done inside or out, it does not matter but you will need space to walk around a central object. Outside obviously allows you to stick your staff or stang into the ground making it slightly easier to use as your focus. Usually this is preceded by hallowing your compass first. If you do not have a stang or staff, you could use a wand, a besom or in fact any object that you can place in the centre that can be used to hold your focus.

Begin to walk around in a circle, keep your eyes set on the central point, but face your body in the direction you are walking. This means your head will be turned to one side as you walk. Try and keep your pace slow and steady to begin with although you may find you do quicken up, go with the flow. You might like to work with a short chant to help the rhythm. As you walk around, keep your eyes focused on the centre. You will begin to feel the energy building and you should naturally begin to enter a trance state. You will feel relaxed and focused. Keep your senses open to whatever or whoever appears to you, it might be visual, it may be words, sounds or emotions, be open to whatever happens. But know that you are ultimately always in control.

You might find you continue to tread the mill whilst you are experiencing the Other world, you may find that you have come to a stop. Once you enter the Other world you may find you drop down to a seated position. There is no right or wrong here.

Once you begin to become aware of your surroundings again, then the journey has come to a natural end. At this point give yourself a few minutes to fully come back to this reality, then ground. It is also advisable to eat and drink something, do not forget to give offerings to the Otherworld spirits at this point to. Each journey experience may well be different, some will take you deep and long, others may not even get you over the threshold. Trust your intuition and know that each one is meant to be whatever it is.

Once you have the hang of treading the mill using the method above it is possible to step into the Otherworld using a simpler method.

Still using your stang, staff or besom but this time sit yourself comfortably in a chair or on the floor. Hold your staff with both hands and place it between your knees/legs in front of you. When you are ready to work tap the staff sharply on the ground. Now close your eyes and focus on your breathing, deep breaths in and deep breaths out. I like to lean the top of the staff towards me, so the wood is touching my forehead. Then you can work with the Elder Mother pathworking I give in this book to begin riding the hedge or devise your own method of stepping into the Other realms using a guided pathworking scenario. Once you have finished your journey come back to your starting point and step back through the veil and into this reality. Obviously, it goes without saying, please do not drive straight after this type of journey. Give yourself time to fully come back to this reality.

28
Hedge Riding Guardian

What I do recommend is finding a guardian to guide you on your hedge riding journeys. This will provide you with support and guidance each time you step into the other realms. I have a lifelong spirit animal guardian, a wild boar who has walked with me for many years. However, when I began to ridge the hedge he refused to come with me. It was even suggested to me that I give him some armour to wear to make him feel more comfortable, but that didn't work. He was adamant that it was not his place to accompany me. On my very first visit however, I was met by a black panther, and he has been my constant companion on each of my hedge riding journeys since.

You may find that your animal guide greets you on your first visit and then each subsequent visit they will be waiting for you. You may even discover the spirit guide crosses over and walks with you on a regular basis whenever you meditate or work magic.

To find or request a spirit animal guide for the other realms you can begin by hallowing the compass or casting a circle and calling in the quarters if you wish. You will need to walk between the worlds to find them. Work with your preferred way of hedge riding using one of the methods within this book.

Once over the hedge follow the guided journey below.

Journey to find a Hedge Riding guardian:

As you step through and out into the other realm, take a look around you. Where are you? What landscape do you see in front of you? What landscape do you see either side of you? They may be different terrains. Which direction are you drawn to take? Choose and begin to walk. As you do so put out the call that you wish to be met by an animal spirit guardian, one that will accompany you on all of your journeys to provide guidance, support and protection. Look, listen and be open to whatever presents itself to you.

If an animal approaches you take some time to connect with and converse with them. Ask them if they are there as your guardian and guide. If they are then take some time to get to know them. If they are not, thank them for their time and keep walking onwards.

It may take more than one journey/visit to find a guardian, if you are tiring then take yourself safely out of the journey and return again at another time. If you find your guardian, once you have spent some time with them, thank them and ask them to meet you at the hedge next time. Then safely take yourself out and return to the here and now.

Your guardian should greet you next time you ride the hedge. Remember this is a relationship so it will take time and effort to build.

29
Entering the Otherworld

You may find that working with the Treading the Mill method takes you straight into the Otherworld at the point you want or need to be in. However, if you prefer to work with pathworking journeys I have given some options here.

The Elder Mother

One of the trees you will find in an English hedgerow is the elder and it carries a long and fascinating history. For me, this is one of the key trees to work with when hedge riding, but you need to know about it and make a connection with the Elder Mother first, because she is a feisty one that can kick your butt without batting an eyelid. The journey script below takes you to greet the Elder Mother and ask for her permission to cross over the boundary.

Elder Mother Journey over the Hedge

Make yourself comfortable somewhere you won't be disturbed. If you prefer you can hallow the compass before working with this exercise. Work with your chosen breath work.

As your world around you dissipates you find yourself standing in a field, long grass grows beneath your feet and the air is fresh around you. The sky above you is bright blue and a host of birds fly overhead. In front of you is a long full hedgerow stretching out to either side for as far as you can see. It is packed full of leafy green plants some with berries, all with different shades and shapes of leaf, some of them are beginning to turn to the colours of autumn. As you look more closely the hedge right in front of you holds a sprawling tree, an elder, deep dark brown earth at the base, roots entangled in the soil surrounded by dead and fallen leaves, insects and fungi. Upwards the elder reaches with several small trunks entwined with each other, branches stretching outwards and merging with the foliage on either side. Bracts of white flowers with a sweet scent sit beside clusters of deep purple black berries dangling from red stalks. Upwards to the top of the hedge where the leaves stretch up into the sky where the birds fly above.

As you stand looking at the elder nestled comfortably within the hedge you hear a faint rustle. Turning you see a figure standing beside the hedge, she had not been there before.

She is the Elder Mother, and you must ask her permission before you enter the hedge and across to the other realms. She turns to look at you, piercing blue eyes seemingly reaching into your soul but with a kindly smile on her face.

You address her:

"Elder Mother, I ask of thee
Permission to cross the boundary
Allow me please to jump the hedge

To enter the Otherworld with respect I pledge"

Then await her answer. If she refuses, then thank her for her time and slowly and gently come back out of the journey. If she grants you access, thank her for her time and turn back to face the hedge and the elder tree within. Where will you enter the elder, which part are you drawn to? Through the roots? Into the twists of the trunk? Or through the leaves at the top?

Where do you feel you need to explore? Feel the soil, smell the earth and the foliage. Make your way through the hedge...

Where are you? Look around, use all your senses, what do you see, feel, hear and smell? On the other side you are met by someone or some creature. It is a person? An animal or something else? They greet you and tell you they are your Otherworld guide.

Let your guide lead you around, take in everything you see, hear and sense. If you have any questions direct them to your guide. If you meet anyone be respectful and use your manners.

When you are finished, ask your guide to lead you back to the hedge. Thank you guide for their time and guidance. Step back through the elder tree in the hedge and through to the other side where you began. If the Elder Mother is still there, thank her again for permission. Then slowly and gently come back to this reality. Open your eyes, wriggle your fingers and toes. Eat and drink something. Make a note of any important details.

The Oak or World Tree Journey

If the idea of the tree as a portal appeals to you, you can use any species of tree, but I think the oak lends itself to the imagery of a large, gnarled and ancient natural portal.

Make yourself comfortable somewhere you won't be disturbed. If you prefer you can hallow the compass before working with this exercise. Work with your chosen breath work.

As your world around you dissipates you find yourself standing just inside the edge of a forest. Looking above you there is a canopy of green foliage with only slight gaps between where the blue skies peep through. Beneath your feet is the forest floor, brown and orange foliage that crunches underfoot.

In front of you is an enormous oak tree, the roots of which are twisted and turning, winding in and out of each other then sinking into the dark brown earth. You notice there is what looks like a gap between some of the roots, as if they have grown to form the entrance to a tunnel.

Looking further up the tree, the trunk is huge, so big you couldn't put your arms around it. The bark is rough and partly covered with moss on one side. In the centre of the trunk the bark has grown around a hole to form a portal into the tree.

Further upwards the branches of the tree spread out over a large distance, reaching across and up, each one covered in masses of green leaves. You realise the higher branches also have what looks like an entrance way, shaped between the leaves. Take your time and look properly at the entire tree, notice the colours, the shapes and the textures of the roots, the bark and the leaves. Now take your gaze to the three portals, the one between the roots, the one in the trunk and then the last one in amongst the branches.

Which one are you drawn to enter?

Address the oak tree, ask for permission to enter the Otherworld. If you receive a positive reply, then make your choice... and crawl or step through the portal. If the tree advises against you entering, give your thanks and slowly come away.

On the other side you are met by someone or some creature.

It is a person? An animal or something else?

They greet you and tell you they are your Otherworld guide. Let your guide lead you around, take in everything you see, hear and sense. If you have any questions direct them to your guide. If you meet anyone be respectful and use your manners.

When you are finished in your journey, make your way back to the oak tree in the Otherworld space, thank your guide and climb back through. Thank the tree for its assistance and then slowly and gently come back to this reality.

Open your eyes, wriggle your fingers and toes and get something to eat and drink to ground yourself.

30
Magical Herbs

One of my favourite areas to work magic with (along with food) are magical herbs and by 'herbs' I mean all plant matter whether it is herbs from the garden, flowering plants, weeds from the hedge rows or trees. The Anglo Saxons called it 'wort cunning' and it translates as 'the knowledge of herbs'. I am an animist which means I believe everything has an energy and by tapping into that energy we can discover what magic it can help us with. Each plant matter will have its own unique and individual energy. There are lists on the internet and in books (including my own!) and I have included some suggestions in this book too. Ultimately you will need to connect with each ingredient you use and get a feel for whether it is right in each case. Trust your intuition, what works for some may not work for others. I like to collect my plant matter from my own garden, if possible, it is free and easily accessible, and I know no pesticides have been used.

The plants will also carry some of my own energy with them. I don't believe in using expensive, exotic ingredients from the other side of the world. Not just because of the eco system aspect, the carbon footprint or the expense, but also because I prefer to use as many plants that are native to my local area as possible.

Local parks, fields and hedgerows are a wonderful resource for foraging, just be careful to correctly identify the plants. Even weeds that grow in the cracks in the pavement in city centres carry magic with them. Local farmers markets and greengrocers are also good suppliers of herbs and spices.

I am lucky enough to have several Asian supermarkets close to me where I can source spices and herbs are reasonable prices if I am looking for something specific. For example, I love working with cinnamon, but there is no way it will grow in my English climate garden, so I do have to outsource on occasion. I collect and dry everything from the garden; seed heads, leaves, bark, flowers, stems, all of it gets harvested, dried, put in jars, labelled and stored.

Within this book I am going to focus on plants that are associated with the hedgerows because it makes sense to focus on the hedge. But remember there are many, many different types of herbs and plants, each one has magical properties whether it is the dandelion pushing up through the crack in the pavement, to the spices and ingredients in your kitchen cupboards.

I would encourage you to seek out local plant life and work with things that are native to your own area if you can, you will feel a stronger energy from them.

Plants also follow the seasons and each season, month in fact each week you will find plants are at different stages and will provide an array of items for you to work with. Even in the darkest, coldest days of winter there will be something in nature to work with. Leaves, flowers, seeds, twigs, bark and roots all carry the magic of a plant or tree. Don't forget the items you have in your kitchen cupboards too, dried herbs, spices and every ingredient you use to cook has magical energy.

Ingesting

I can't reiterate this enough, if you are intending to ingest the herb or plant you have collected, please make sure you have identified it correctly and that it is not harmful in any way.

Safety

Please do not give herbal mixtures to pregnant women, babies or young children unless you are 100% sure it is safe for them to use. Herbs are considered to be safe because they are natural. However, whilst they are safer than many chemical medicines, this is only true if they are used properly. Inappropriate use of some herbs could be dangerous; this includes combining them with prescription medicines or using them to treat a serious illness without consulting a doctor.

Illness

If the illness you are intending to treat with herbal remedies is major, please get a professional diagnosis and let your practitioner know what remedies you intend to take. Some herbal remedies can react badly to modern medicines.

Cleanliness

When preparing herbal remedies please keep everything spotless, your work surfaces, jars you keep the herbs in, your hands, any utensils you use. If you are intending to make and use herbal remedies it is advisable to have at least a basic understanding of the human body and how it works. This will enable you to distinguish symptoms common to an illness. And to know when to refer to a conventional practitioner.

Harvesting

Only buy or harvest what you need. If you are gathering your herbs in the wild or from your garden, only take what you need, leave enough on the plant for it to survive. Herbs do not keep forever so don't have huge stocks; even dried herbs don't last indefinitely.

Storage

If you are drying your own herbs, or if you have purchased them dried, keep them in a cool place out of sunlight. Dark glass jars are the best form of storage vessel. If you dry your own herbs, make sure you do so correctly so that they don't rot and make sure they are properly labelled with the plant name and date you collected it.

From the wild

If you do forage in the wild, please, please make sure you can correctly identify the plant that you are harvesting, or the results could be disastrous. Please also make sure that the plant you are intending to harvest from is not protected or endangered. Do make sure you only take a little of the plant and leave enough for it to survive properly. Make sure the plant is not near any fields that have been sprayed with pesticide or near car fumes.

Ethical Wildcrafting

Before we go any further, I would like to just mention here for any items whether they are seeds, buds, sticks or feathers try to use items that have been gifted rather than plucking feathers from a live bird (which would probably be difficult and dangerous anyway) and use sticks and leaves that have fallen to the ground rather than cutting them from the tree or plant.

Ethical wildcrafting is the practice of harvesting plants and trees conscientiously, to avoid damaging the health of the plant population or the overall ecological system. With seeds and fruits maybe just make sure you ask the plant first if it is OK for you to harvest the fruits and leave an offering in place. Please don't take more than you need, leave enough for others, for animals and birds and in the case of seeds for the plant to reseed itself. Make sure to only take a small amount and leave enough of the plant in situ so that it can continue to grow. Please also note that some plants in the wild are protected and even on the verge of extinction.

How to harvest:

If you are picking flowers or plants for magical workings, then here is a basic guide: If you can collect fallen flowers, seeds, twigs etc.

then even better because the plant is already done with them but if you want to remove them directly from the plant always be careful not to damage the plant itself, only take what you need, leave enough of the plant left to continue growing and always ask permission from the plant first. Use a sharp knife or cutters, blunt blades leave jagged edges which can leave the plant open to infection.

Flowers

It is usually best to pick flowers when the bud is fully open and cut the stalk at the first leaf joint. If possible, pick them in the morning before the sun gets too hot. To dry them lay them out on kitchen towel in a warm dry place (I put them on trays in the conservatory). Once dried store them in a dark glass jar with a detailed label (what they are and the date you harvested them). The dark glass prevents fading from sunlight.

Seeds

Seed harvesting should be done on a dry day; you don't want to take home seed heads that are all soggy from the rain because they will go mouldy. Once seed pods have changed from green to brown and can be easily split, you can begin collecting flower seeds. Cut the pod or seed head from the stalk and pop into a paper bag. Or you can hang seed heads on stalks upside down with a paper bag tied around to catch the seeds.

Bark

You can successfully harvest small amounts of bark direct from the tree, birch trees in particular lend themselves to this practise without suffering too much but...and here's the thing, I can never bring myself to strip bark direct from a tree. I do however pick up pieces of fallen bark or strip bark from branches that have been removed by forest wardens or that perhaps a storm has knocked down. If you don't harvest bark properly, you can kill the tree. If you want to give it a try it is best to only do so in the autumn when the tree is starting to prepare for winter and is drawing all its energy into the core. Depending on how much bark you need you can just shave a little piece direct from the tree or cut a small branch off and use all the bark from that. But do your research first, identify the type of tree as there are different methods for different trees – Google should be able to help you with the finer details.

Roots

To harvest roots from a plant first of all check that it is a healthy looking plant and that you have identified it correctly. Some people find the largest plant or what they call 'the grandmother plant' and ask permission to harvest some roots, if the answer comes back as a yes then you can harvest one or two of the smaller plants that surround the grandmother. Roots are best gathered in spring or early autumn.

Although I personally think autumn is best because the plant has been allowed to grow, flower and spread seed over the summer. Dig the plant out carefully and if possible, just trim pieces of the root from the ends and then pop the plant back into the earth. If this isn't possible then please make sure there are plenty of others from the species growing in the surrounding areas. Once you get them home wash off as much soil as you can then dry them well. To dry roots out I find that chopping them into smaller pieces works best then lay them out on a flat tray and put in a dry, dark place. When they are completely dried, they will feel dry to the touch but still be slightly spongy. Store in dark glass jars with detailed labels.

Leaves

If you are harvesting herbs then it is best to pick them in the morning and either tie them into bundles and hang them up or lay them out separately on trays in a dry, dark place (leaving them in sunshine fades the colour). For plant leaves such as trees or wild plants you can look in the autumn for fallen leaves which will already be dry, or you can pick them directly from the plant or tree. Be careful not to tear or rip them from the plant, just gently pluck each one. Then lay them out to dry. For a lot of the fresh green plant leaves they usually keep their colour and dry better if you harvest them direct from the plant or tree in the spring. Again, store in dark glass jars as sunlight can fade them.

Berries

Now these are a bit trickier to dry, with something like a blackberry you are probably better picking them ripe and eating them straight away or they freeze well. If you want to use blackberry in magical workings, then go for the petals of the flower or the leaves. Leave the fruit for yummy puddings. However, berries from the hawthorn for instance are much easier to dry, pick them ripe thread them onto a string using a needle then hang them up to dry.

Charging

Any ingredient used in spell working needs to be charged with your intent. This goes for herbs, spices and candles. Take the item in your hand and visualise your goal, see the result playing out in your mind's eye and send that energy into the ingredient. Tell the item what you need it to do, it needs clear instructions, and this is where the verbal charm comes into play. You need to programme the items in your spell working.

Simples

A simple is a term that refers to the use of a single herb and often in the form of an herbal tea. Herbal tea is one of the most simple (pun intended) magical items to create with herbs.

A general guide for a simple:
One heaped teaspoon dried herbs
One cup of boiling water

Steep the herbs for five to ten minutes, say your charm whilst the herbs are brewing and then drink. Simples can be added to a bucket or bowl of water and used as floor or surface washes for cleaning your house as well.

Oils

Oil blends are incredibly useful in magical workings, the essential oils you purchase have gone through a complicated process and they usually have a strong scent. If purchasing these be mindful to check they are pure essential oils with no additives or chemical scents. You can make your own infused oils which is easy to do, they have a powerful magic, but usually do not have such a strong scent. Most essential oils should be diluted if they are going to be used topically. Using a 2% dilution is considered a safe guideline and if using oils on the elderly or children this should be further reduced to 1%. (Please consult a qualified aromatherapist if considering using oils on children as many are not safe to use.) The essential oil should be diluted using a carrier oil, sometimes called a base oil. An example of a base oil is coconut, olive or almond oil.

First choose a base/carrier oil from the list above preferably one that has a mild scent like olive oil. Next choose flowers, herbs, spices and citrus peel to use in your oil. Cut the flowers just before they are fully open and where possible, use the petals only. You can use a single type of flower or a mixture of 2 or more flowers. Herbs: Almost any garden herb can be used to make essential oils such as marjoram, peppermint, lemon verbena, lemon balm and rosemary. Cut the herbs just before the flowers open. Use the leaves and flowers, but not the woody stems. Chop the leaves before adding into the oil. Spices can also be used. Use a pestle or mortar to crush them before adding them to oil. The zest of citrus fruits can be used to make homemade essential oils. Use them sparingly in mixtures. About 2-3 strips of zest per bottle.

The easiest method to make essential oils is by enfleurage and maceration. Enfleurage is a method that involves steeping the plants in cool olive oil. After some time, the oil strained off and the plants are replaced with fresh ones. This process is repeated until the strength of the aroma of oils meets your requirements.

Maceration is the same method as above except that the container of the oil is placed in hot water for a few hours each day to speed up the process.

Method 1

You will need:

1-piece 600ml wide necked jar with tight fitting lid
300 ml oil
Glass mixing bowl
Muslin (to cover the top of the bowl)
Dark glass bottle with tight fitting lid or stopper
8 tablespoon of flower petals
6 tablespoons of chopped herbs (optional)
4 tablespoons of crushed spices (optional)
6 tablespoons of thinly pared citrus zest (optional)

Note: The amount of the plant materials needs to be renewed several times. So, prepare that in double or triple amounts.

Put the oil into the jar then add the plant material and stir. Cover tightly and leave for 48 hours in a sunny windowsill, shaking every 12 hours. Lay a piece of muslin over the bowl and strain the oils. Gather up the muslin and squeeze the material to extract as much as you can. Put the oil back to the jar and add fresh material. Continue in a same way until you get the aroma you want. After final straining, you can put the oil into a dark glass bottled. The shelf life for your essential oil is 6 - 12 months if kept in a dry, dark, cool place.

Method 2 (this method is better if you are using petals such as rose)
You will need:
8 cups (large handfuls) petals, herbs and/or spices
1 cup/236ml base oil
Pot
4 cups/946ml water
Glass jar
Pestle
Sieve

Bring 4 cups of water to a boil, then remove it from heat. Put 1 cup of your chosen base oil in a glass jar. Set the glass jar with the oil in the pan of hot water. This will keep the oil warm, which helps it pull the scent from the plant matter. Shred or crush 1 cup of petals or your chosen plant matter with a pestle in a glass bowl. You can also use a wooden spoon or your fingers if you have no other supplies available.

Place the plant matter in the jar with the oil and cover. Once the pan of water cools, you can move the jar to a warm, sunny windowsill.

Leave the oil and plant matter alone for at least 24 hours. We recommend letting the petals to soak in oil for up to 7 days, depending upon how strong of a scent you desire. Remove the plant matter from the oil and squeeze them to get all of the oil into the jar. Strain the oil through a fine mesh sieve into another jar or glass bowl to remove any petal pieces or other debris. Repeat Steps 1 through 8 for a minimum of 7 days. Store the finished oil in a dark glass jar, or a glass jar kept in a dark cupboard.

PLEASE DO YOU RESEARCH BEFORE MAKING ANY OILS – SOME CAN BE INCREDIBLY TOXIC.
NEVER USE AN ESSENTIAL OIL DIRECT ON YOUR SKIN WITHOUT FIRST DILUTING WITH A BASE OIL.

NEVER INGEST ESSENTIAL OIL WITHOUT CONSULTING A QUALIFIED PRACTITIONER.

When making your own essential oil blend I use the following rule of thumb:

10ml base oil
20-25 drops essential oil

If I am creating a blend to use in an oil burner, I omit the base oil. Before you go tipping drops of essential oil into others I do a test first, then you don't create a blend you hate. Take a small slip of card or paper towel and put a drop of the first essential oil you want to use on it, sniff to see if you like it, if you do then add a drop of the next oil followed by the sniff test again, repeat until you have a blend you like. Or if you realise you don't like it you can start again and you won't have wasted lots of oil. Keep things simple, as a guide I tend to use three sometimes four different oils, never more than that otherwise it gets complicated.

Incense

Incense has been used throughout history by many cultures and for various reasons. The obvious reason perhaps being to make the air smell sweeter. It is also used to cleanse the area from negative energy, to invite spirits and deity in, to honour the gods, to clear the air during funerary rites and as an offering. It can be used to help you transition into another state or realm.

Smoke from incense is useful to cleanse and charge amulets and spell pouches too. In fact, I think the use of incense as an offering is greatly under rated. Incense creates a scene; it works with our senses to help our subconscious reach a different level.

Creating your own magical incense blend is easy, experiment and see what creations work best for you. Loose incense blends are good to burn on charcoal discs but equally work well added to the top of an oil burner, the latter gives the magical scent but not the smoke. I pop a small amount of sand in the top of the oil burner before adding the loose incense, then it doesn't melt to the bottom of the dish. Do bear in mind that not all incense blends will smell wonderful. If you are going for the intent of the ingredients in the blend it won't necessarily have a delightful scent.

My rule of thumb for a good incense blend is:

A resin – made from tree sap, this burns for longer, but bear in mind it does produce smoke if you put it on charcoal.

A woody herb – helps the blend to burn longer.

A leafy herb – burns quickly.

A spice – powdered spice burns quickly; woody spice burns for longer.

A few drops of essential oil – helps to add a stronger scent.
You can create a blend using just one or two of the above ingredients, but a mixture of all of them provides a long burning blend and one that has a good scent. You can of course use incense sticks and cones or bundles of dried herbs. Remember to charge each ingredient with your intent as you blend it.

A note of caution. Be mindful of the type of ingredients you are burning; some herbs produce toxic smoke.

My personal Hedge Riding loose incense blend is a mixture of:

Cinnamon bark
Star Anise
Cloves
Juniper berries
Cardamon
Bay
Pine resin

I add a pinch of each and then give them a quick grind in the mortar and pestle just to break them up a bit, I do not grind it to a powder, keep it roughly broken. This is also the mixture I use to dress my Hedge Riding candle; I just grind the ingredients much finer.

Herb bundles

Herb bundles are easy to make, and I would encourage you to step outside the usual bundle of white sage and experiment with herbs that are native to your location. You will also find that different herbs produce different results particularly when cleansing the home from negative energy. I like to use herbs such as lavender, mugwort and rosemary. Cut fresh herbs giving a decent length of stalk and tie them into a tight bundle with string or twine (make sure it will burn safely). Wind the twine around the whole length of the bundle, up and down, criss crossing the twine as you go. The bundle will then need to be left in a dry place to dry out, you may need to tighten the twine once it is dried as the herbs can shrink. I have made these using pre dried herbs, you follow the same process with the twine, and it does work, but the herbs are more fragile and do crumble a bit, but you create an herb bundle without the need to wait for it to dry out.

The herb bundle can then be lit with a flame, allow the herbs to catch then blow out the flame so you are left with a smoking herb bundle. Waft the smoke around your home, your body or magical tools to cleanse the area from negative energy.

Mists

Room and body mist sprays are easy to make and can be used for magical purpose to cleanse a room or bring in a magical energy.

Basic recipe:

180ml/6 fl oz distilled water
24 drops essential oil
Sprig of herbs, pinch of flower petals or spices

Distilled water is just boiled water from your kettle, allowed to cool. Pour the water into a spray bottle then add the oils and plant matter. Spray the mist around your house or over your body.

Potions

These are mixtures of herbs added to water, oil, alcohol or vinegar. These can be taken internally for medicinal use if the herbs are safe, but I tend to use them regularly for magical purpose. If you are intending to ingest any herbals, please do make sure you have identified the plant matter correctly and make sure it does not interfere with any medication you currently take or adversely affect any health issues you might have. Be safe, not sorry, herbals can be incredibly powerful, and some are quite toxic to ingest.

A potion can be used to: Sprinkle on your altar, magical tools or spell pouches. Dress candles. Anoint yourself before working magic. Made into sprays to cleanse the room or your body. Created as a liquid to mark a sacred space. Add to your bath water. Use essential oil blends in an oil burner. Add essential oil to a small jar of salt and use to sniff from when you need a boost.

Decoction

This is a good way to use plant bark, berries and roots. Chop fresh or dried herb and simmer in water for about 20 minutes. Strain and then drink. This can also be used as a mouth wash or gargle. (Only keep for a maximum of 48 hours).

Use 1 heaped teaspoon of chopped herb material to 1 ½ cups/350ml water.

Tincture

These are made by macerating (which means soaking) chopped herbs from any part of the plant in an alcohol solution. Sometimes vinegar or glycerol is used instead of alcohol. The ratio of herb to water and alcohol will determine the strength of the tincture but the most common ratio is 1-part herb to 3 parts water and alcohol. The proportion of alcohol varies from 25 per cent to 90 per cent. Tinctures do have a long shelf life but usually take at least a week to prepare. Place the chopped herb material in a clean, preferably sterilised jar and stir in the required amount of alcohol. For each 4oz/113g of dried herb material add ½ pint/284ml of alcohol solution. Stir, then close with a lid, leave for 10 days, make sure to shake the jar every day.

After 10 days strain and put into a clean bottle. Vodka is the preferred alcohol to use, but I have successfully used whisky too. Fresh plant material needs a 40 per cent alcohol solution. Dried plant material can be made with 25 per cent alcohol. If it is below 25 per cent the tincture may decay.

Hot infused oil is only used externally. You need to put your fresh herbs in a jar and cover with oil – olive, almond or sunflower. Put the jar in a saucepan of water up to its neck and bring the water to a simmer for 3 hours. Then strain into a brown glass bottle.

Cold infused oils are made in a similar way but instead of heating in a saucepan of water you put the jar on a sunny windowsill instead.

An ointment covers and protects the skin; a good base for an ointment is petroleum jelly or beeswax pellets. The jelly or wax is melted in a double boiler and herbs are added, simmered until they are crisp and strained into jars.

A cream is made from oil, beeswax and water and this penetrates the skin. Melt 1oz/28g beeswax in a double boiler; add 1 cup/236ml olive oil and mix. Add 2oz /56g of your chosen herb. (If it's too thick add a small amount of water and mix). Simmer for 20 minutes, stirring. Add a drop of benzoin to preserve. Then strain into sterilized jars.

31
Into the Hedge

> ¹'The divelish hag by chaunges of my cheare
> Perceiv'd my thought, and drownd in sleepie night,
> With wicked herbs and ointments did besmeare
> My body all, through charms and magicke might,
> That all my senses were bereaved quight:'

In this section I want to delve into the hedgerow to look closely at the plant life you would find there and the magic it has to offer. Each plant can provide a magical connection and be used in spell work. Most of them can also be used in incense or oil blends too.

This information may also be useful to guide you to seek out a particular plant spirit if you feel drawn to. You can set an intent before you begin your hedge riding to meet a certain plant spirit, make sure you set the scene and landscape to that which the plant grows in. You may find you just meet and interact with the energy of the plant, but you might also find you are greeted by a plant spirit that appears to you in a human form. The Elder Mother plant spirit always appears to me as a little old lady, but each plant has its own unique and individual character. Be open to whatever or whoever you meet. Obviously, this is just a very small

---

1   Faery Queene, Edmund Spenser, 16th C

mall selection, do investigate your local area and see what you can find. Just be careful to make sure you have identified them properly and check whether they are toxic in any way and are safe to touch and/or burn.

Blackberry (rubus fruticosus)

'"Brambles of Mordor were ugly with foot-long thorns, which were sharp as the knives of the orcs that came from Mordor. Some of the thorns were long and sharp, meaning that they could puncture very deeply, while others were barbed, making them suited for rending the flesh if one tried to walk through them. They sprawled over the land like coils of steel wire.'

Other names: By, bramble, bramble-kite, bumble-kite, bremelberie, black heg

The blackberry can often be found in wild hedgerows, and it makes a safe and secure habit for wildlife. The growth of the plant often produces branches shaped as archways and folklore loves these. [2]Those who were ill need only crawl through a blackberry arch from east to west to remove their pain and disease.

Many folk stories advise not picking blackberries later in the year as the devil has either spat or peed on them, this does actually make sense as the fruit is susceptible to fungus in the autumn.

---

1   Lord of the Rings, J R R Tolkien
2   Witch's Garden, Sandra Lawrence

The fruit can be eaten to imbue the magical properties but for magical use in spell work I use the thorns and the leaves; it is less messy.

Parts used in magic: Leaves, thorns
Blackberries Magical Properties: Prosperity, protection, fertility, Faerie
Ruling planet – Venus
Element – Water, Fire, Earth
Energy – Feminine

Blackthorn
(Prunus spinosa)

[1]"The twa appear'd like sisters twin,
In feature, form, an' claes;
Their visage wither'd, lang an' thin,
An' sour as only slaes'

Other names: Dark Crone of the Woods, slae, sloe

The blackthorn has long been associated with witchcraft and magic and has strong connections to the winter goddess, The Cailleach and was considered to be a keeper of secrets. [2]The thorns of the blackthorn were believed to be used by witches to prick wax poppets, in fact I still use them for this and to pin and carve candles. Blackthorn wands and staffs were often held by those in high office, such as the Sergeant at Arms in the House of Lords in England.

---

1   The Holy Fair, Robert Burns, 1785
2   Witch's Garden, Sandra Lawrence

Some folk tales include a blackthorn stone being thrown behind the hero, when it hits the ground a hedge instantly grows to stop the baddies from following.

Parts used in magic: Thorns, leaves, wood, stones from the fruit (sloe)
Blackthorn Magical Properties: Protection, exorcism, divination, healing

Ruling planet – Saturn and Mars
Sign - Scorpio
Element – Fire
Energy – Masculine

Cramp Bark/Guelder Rose (Vibrunum opulus)

[1]'Walk not amidst guelder-rose and sloes when the evening air is still warm
A miraculous daemon dwells in the dusky room of the trees...
Avoid sloe and guelder-rose and the false song of the thickets'

Other names: Snowball tree, queen's cushion, Whitsun boss, May ball, tisty-tosty, club branches. Parts used in magic: Flowers, berries, leaves, bark

[2]The Guelder Rose features in a lot of Slavic myths and legends and is associated with the birth of the Universe and the 'fire

---

1   Häxorna/The Witches, Erik Axel Karlfelt
2   Forest Farm Peace Gardening

trinity' which consists of the sun, the moon and the star. The berries symbolise home and family. [1]A folk tale from Scandinavia refers to the guelder rose as 'water elder' which was used by a water spirit called Nix, who would wait beneath the plant whilst playing beautiful music. When a passerby stopped to listen, the Nix would jump up and pull them under the water, unless they were protected by carrying a piece of guelder rose in their pocket.

Cramp Bark Magical Properties: Relaxing, meditation, stress, tension, anxiety, healing, rebirth, protection
Element – Earth
Energy – Feminine

Dandelion
(Taraxacum officinale)

[2]'Dear common flower, that grow'st beside the way,
Fringing the dusty road with harmless gold,
First pledge of blithesome May,
Which children pluck, and, full of pride uphold,
High-hearted buccaneers, o'erjoyed that they
An Eldorado in the grass have found,
Which not the rich earth's ample round
May match in wealth, thou art more dear to me
Than all the prouder summer-blooms may be.'

Other names: Piss-a-bed, Gaming of the fields, lion's tooth, Bearnan Bride, blowball, priest's crown

---

1 Bug Woman London
2 To The Dandelion, James Russell Lowell, mid 1800s

One of the first flowers in the year for the bees to feed on, so please don't weed them out! The seeds are packed full of wish magic and the whole plant can be eaten, the roots made into a coffee substitute (although I think it tastes like dirt) and the flowers make a very decent wine.

In Scotland the Gaelic name for the dandelion is 'Bearnan Bride' which translates to mean 'little notched of Bride' connecting the plant with the goddess/saint, Brighid.

Parts used in magic: Seeds, flowers, leaves, roots
Dandelion Magical Properties: Wishes, divination, love, abundance, psychic powers
Ruling planet –Jupiter
Sign - Taurus
Element – Air
Energy – Masculine

Elder
(Sambucus spp)

[1]'Lady Elder
Give me some of thy wood
Then will I give thee some of mine
When I become a tree'

Other names: Danewort, walewort, blood hilder, the name 'elder' may come from the Anglo-Saxon word 'aeld' with means 'fire', the

---

[1]   A prayer from Lower Saxony

hollowed out stems of the tree were used to blow on kindling to light fires.

In Scandinavian and German legends, the Elder Mother (Hyldemöer) lives within the plant. Her permission must be sought if you wish to pick or cut anything from the tree. You must chant your request three times whilst down on bended knee. If the proper etiquette is not followed there would be consequences, unpleasant ones. To burn the wood of an elder tree is also believed to bring about disaster and even death.

[1] A lot of old stories and folk tales refer to it as 'wicked wood' or 'witch wood' and it was rarely used to make anything with. Although witches were believed to use the wood to bring about a storm by stirring a bucket of water with a twig from the elder tree. It was also believed that a witch could turn themselves into an elder tree. Stories from Ireland tell of witches riding elder branches rather than broomsticks.

[2] It is said the plant flourishes everywhere in England that Danish blood was split during the centuries of struggle with the Vikings which explains the name 'danewort'.

[3] One old recipe suggests ritually killing the plant during darkness and leaving it transfixed by the lethal knife until it is exposed to both the full light of sun and the holy power of the altar.

---

1   Discovering the Folklore of Plants, Margaret Baker
2   Leechcraft, Stephen Pollington
3   Medicinale Anglicum/Bald's Leechbook, 10th Century

Grow an elder beside your front door and it will protect your house from evil, lightening and witchcraft and bring fertility. If you find an elder that has self-seeded in your garden this is believed to be lucky.

Elderberries gathered on St John's Eve[1] would give you magical powers. [2]Elder given to the bewitched on St John's Eve would break the spell. [3]Musical instruments used by the Fair Folk were said to be made from elder wood. In fact, the wood from the elder tree has a soft core which can be removed to create hollow pipes, so it lends itself to wind instruments very well.

Parts used in magic: Flowers, berries, leaves, wood, roots
Elder Magical Properties: Protection, healing, faeries, purification, intuition, exorcism, hex breaking, rebirth
Ruling planet – Venus
Sign – Sagittarius, Aquarius, Libra
Element – Water
Energy – Feminine

Hawthorn (Crataegus spp)

[4]'The hawthorn's bloom is falling, love
We must no longer wait
Each bird is blithely calling, love
Unto his chosen mate'

---
1 St John's Eve is celebrated on 23rd June.
2 Plant Lore & Legend, Ruth Binney
3 Treesforlife.org.uk
4 John Ingham, 19th C

Other names: Hag-thorn, quickthorn, hedge thorn

The thorns of the hawthorn are particularly useful in magic and the flowers herald the arrival of the festival of Beltane and May Day and therefore fertility and love. The hawthorn forms a triad with the oak and the ash which offer a gateway to the fairy world.

[1]'In some parts a branch of hawthorn was burnt on New Year's morning to support a good harvest for the coming year, the remains of the wood were kept until the next year. Bringing the flowers into the house was thought to bring the omen of death or the plague as the flowers were thought to have the scent of death. Hawthorn wood makes very good divining rods.

[2]'Pick a piece of hawthorn at midnight on the Twelfth Night and bring it indoors to bring you good luck.'

If you need to fell a hawthorn you must first offer the plant a prayer and give an explanation to the plant spirit (to be fair this practice should follow with all plants and trees), if you don't follow this etiquette then awful misfortune will befall you. Felling of a hawthorn must only be a last resort, if you are cutting the tree down to build a house then misfortune for those that live there is apparently unavoidable. Hawthorn has a link to the crown of thorns worn by Jesus Christ, and it is this connection which may have given hawthorn the healing reputation.

---

1   Witch's Garden, Sandra Lawrence
2   Discovering the Folk Law of Plants, Margaret Baker

Parts used in magic: Flowers, berries, leaves, thorns, wood, roots
Hawthorn Magical Properties: Happiness, fertility, love, protection, purification, forgiveness, faeries, hope

Ruling planet – Mars, Venus
Sign - Sagittarius
Element – Fire
Energy – Masculine

Mugwort
(Artemisia vulgaris)

[1]'Be mindful, Mugwort, what you revealed,
What you established at the Great Proclamation
Una you are called, oldest of herbs,
you are strong against three and against thirty,
you are strong against poison and against [flying venoms]
you are strong against the foe who goes through the land.'

Other names: Midgewort, common wormwood, chrysanthemum weed, cronewort, sailor's tobacco

From [2]OE Herbarium MS V: "when someone wishes to begin a journey, have him take this herb artemisia in his hand and have it with him, then he will not find the journey too great; and also it drives off demonic possession and in the house where he has it inside, it forbids evil leechdoms and also it averts the eyes of evil men".

---
1   Lacnunga, Anglo Saxon texts
2   Leechcraft, Stephen Pollington

The plant should be picked before sunrise with a short magical invocation [1]'tollam te artemisia ne lassus sum in via', that it should be hallowed with the sign of the cross as it is picked. Then it can be held or put in the shoe of the traveller. Mugwort was used during the Iron Age to flavour drinks, including beer.

Parts used in magic: Leaves, flowers
Mugwort Magical Properties: Strength, psychic powers, protection, dreams, healing, astral travel, feminine energy, cleansing

Ruling planet – Venus, Moon
Sign - Cancer
Element – Earth
Gender – Feminine

Rowan
(Sorbus acuparia)

[2]'Oh! rowan tree, oh! rowan tree,
Thou'lt aye be dear to me,
En twin'd thou art wi' mony ties
O' hame and infancy.
Thy leaves were aye the first o' spring,
Thy flow'rs the simmer's pride;
There was na sic a bonnie tree
In a' the countrie side.

---

1   Roughly translated as 'I will take you so that I am not tired on the way'
2   The Rowan Tree, Carolina Oliphant (Lady Nairne) 1822

Oh! rowan tree.'

Other names: Lady of the mountain, quicken tree, wildwood, whispering tree

Berries of the rowan tree have a tiny five-pointed star shape at the base, a pentagram perhaps? [1] Rowan trees have often been thought of as the 'witches tree' with dark connotations, but also a tree of the Fair Folk. The rowan brings protection, and the wood was traditional used to make cradles and coffins. Rowan is mentioned in several stories of deities such as the goddess Hebe from Greek mythology and the Norse god Thor. Celtic tales suggest the first woman was created from the rowan tree, the first man from an ash. Folk would carry a small piece about their person to ward against witches, pieces of rowan were also attached to the horns of cattle for protection.

Parts used for magic: Berries, leaves, flowers, wood
Rowan Magical Properties: Psychic powers, power, success, protection, love, spirituality, faeries, divination, healing, inspiration

Ruling planet – Sun, Mercury
Sign - Sagittarius
Element – Fire
Energy – Masculine

---

[1] Witch's Garden, Sandra Lawrence

Stinging Nettle
(Urtica dioica)

[1]'With her soft hands she took hold of the dreadful nettles that seared like fire.

Great blisters rose on her hands and arms, but she endured it gladly in the hope that she could free her beloved brothers. She crushed each nettle with her bare feet and spun the green flax.'

Other names: Devil of a fellow, naughty man's plaything, Devil's apron

We are all familiar with the humble stinging nettle which grows wild everywhere. Nettles are edible and can be spun into a very decent string and cloth. [2]In fact, folklore says the devil collects stinging nettles on May Day to make into his shirts, not that he would have need for a shirt though. The nettle has a history of being a protective plant against evil and witchcraft, which is just plain rude really. A healer could apparently cure a fever by pulling a nettle up out of the ground, roots and all whilst speaking out loud the name of their patient and the parent's names as well.

Nettle is included as one of the nine sacred herbs of Odin charm, mentioned in a 10th Century manuscript.

Parts used in magic: Leaves, stalks
Nettle Magical Properties: Healing, protection, lust, money, ex-

---
1   The Wild Swans, Hans Christian Anderson
2   Witch's Garden, Sandra Lawrence

orcism.

Ruling planet – Mars
Sign – Scorpio, Aries
Element – Fire
Energy – Masculine

Wormwood
(Artemisia absinthium)

[1]'But as with children, when physicians try to administer rank wormwood, they first touch the rims about the cups with the sweet yellow fluid of honey, that unthinking childhood be deluded as far as the lips, and meanwhile may drink up the bitter juice of the wormwood, and though beguiled be not betrayed, but rather by such means be restored and regain health, so now do I: since this doctrine commonly seems somewhat harsh to those who have not used it and the people shrink back from it, I have chosen to set forth our doctrine to you in sweet-speaking Pierian song, and as it were to touch it with the Muses' delicious honey.'

Other names: Ware-moth, old woman

The Latin 'Artemisia' is a nod to the Greek goddess, Artemis. It was used for various medicinal purposes but also burned along with sandalwood to help contact the spirit world. [2]Mixed with the herb mugwort, together they were used to 'conjure spirits'. It is the key ingredient in the drink absinthe nicknamed 'the green fairy',

---

1   De rerum natura, Titus Lucretius Carus, mid 90s-50s BCE
2   Witch's Garden, Sandra Lawrence

which was highly potent and produced hallucinogenic effects if drunk frequently. [1]Apparently, the artists Van Gogh and Picasso were partial to a glass or two of absinthe, which explains some of their artwork.

[2]Wormwood is said to have flourished in the Garden of Eden, wherever the serpent's path went. The key feature of wormwood is the very bitter taste.

Parts used in magic: Leaves
Wormwood Magical Properties: Vengeance, attack magic, protection, divination, dreams, meditation, psychic powers

Ruling planet – Mars, Moon
Sign – Cancer, Scorpio
Element – Fire
Energy – Masculine

Yarrow
(Achillea millefolium)

[3]'I will pluck the yarrow fair
That more benign will be my face,
That more warm shall be my lips,
That more chaste shall be my speech,
Be my speech the beams of the sun,
Be my lips the sap of the strawberry.

1	Healthline.com
2	Discovering the Folklore of Plants, Margaret Baker
3	Carmina Gadelica Alexander Carmichael, 19th C

May I be an isle in the sea,
May I be a hill on the shore,
May I be a star in the waning of the moon,
May I be a staff to the weak.
Wound can I every man,
Wound can no man me.'

Other names: Knight's milfoil, staunch weed, solder's woundwort, sneezewort, nosebleed, carpenter's plant, old man's pepper, seven years love

[1]The name Achillea was given by [2]Carl Linnaeus in honour of the Greek hero, Achilles. The name yarrow is Anglo Saxon, from 'gearwe'. [3]There are variations on the translation, but suggestions are it means 'spear' or 'armour'. Throwing yarrow over your threshold keeps witches away (apparently). Leaves of the yarrow were eaten at weddings to ensure the couple stayed together for at least seven years. Leaves of yarrow held over the eyes was believed to give the gift of second sight. The stalks of yarrow were used in the Chinese divination method of iChing.

A lot of the folk names and myths refer to yarrow as being able to staunch wounds or stop bleeding from blade wounds.

Parts used in magic: Flowers, leaves, root
Yarrow Magical Properties: Psychic powers, love, courage, exorcism, dreams, peace, happiness, divination, protection. Ruling planet – Venus. Element- Water. Gender-Feminine

1   Witch's Garden, Sandra Lawrence
2   Swedish biologist, 1707-1778
3   Anglo-Saxon Dictionary, John R Clark Hall, 1916

32
Flying Ointment

[1]"Granny Weatherwax was in trouble. First, she decided, she should never have allowed Hilta to talk her into borrowing her broomstick. It was elderly, erratic, would fly only at night and even then couldn't manage a speed much above a trot. Its lifting spells had worn so thin that it wouldn't even begin to operate until it was already moving at a fair lick. It was, in fact, the only broomstick ever to need bump-starting. And it was while Granny Weatherwax, sweating and cursing, was running along a forest path holding the damn thing at shoulder height for the tenth time that she had found the bear trap.'

The idea of a witch flying about on a broomstick seems to have been around for a few centuries. The earliest known image shows three witches each of them with the head of an animal, all riding forked branches. The image was an engraving entitled De Lamiis, by Ulrich Molitor in 1489. Part of the witch on a broomstick lore is that of the flying ointment, the first written mention of that was in 1456 by Johannes Hartlieb, mentioned later in 1507 by theologian Alfonso Tostado in his writings Super Genesis Commentaria. A story from 1477 was given by Antone Rose who claimed the devil gave her a long stick on which she was to run

---

1   Equal Rites, Terry Pratchett, 1987

an ointment, then she was to shout go' and she would be able to fly through the air on the stick. The power of flying ointment is mentioned in the 1525 publication Tractatus de strigibus sive maleficis (treatise on witches or evildoers). Witch trials from 1664 in Somerset make reference to the use of flying ointment which was apparently greenish in colour and was to be anointed on the body and followed with the words 'thout, tout a tout, tout, throughout and about' and then to return the phrase 'rentum tormentum'. Interestingly if you put this phrase into a modern Latin translator it comes up with 'rent a gun', I am fairly certain that wasn't the original meaning! Another suggestion for translation is [1]"kiss of death". These don't make a lot of sense, breaking it down the word [2]"tormentum' translates to mean 'instrument for twisting and winding, or torture'. Most online translators give 'rentum' as meaning 'rent', I wonder if the phrase has been misheard and twisted over time?

What were the ingredients in these infamous flying ointments? Recipes have appeared in various texts such as the Magia Naturalis from 1558. In 1436, Johannes Nider in his Formicarius wrote that boiled, unbaptised babies were the main ingredient. In Discoverie of Witchcraft from 1584, Reginald Scot wrote that bowels and members of children dug from their graves were boiled in a cauldron to create a grease used in the flying ointment. In the Sylva Sylvarum from 1608 written by Lord Veralum (Francis Bacon) writes: 'The ointment that witches use is reported to be made from the fat of children dug out of their graves; of the juices of smallage, wolf bane, and cinque-foil, mingled with the meal of fine wheat. But I suppose that the soporifer-

---

1 https://mymemory.translated.net/
2 Oxford Latin Dictionary

- ous medicines are likest to do it' which are henbane, hemlock, mandrake, moonshade, tobacco, opium, saffron, poplar leaves'. I suspect the use of fat, more likely to have been lard rather than from babies obviously, was to create a useable cream base. The idea of babies being used would probably have come from the Church as a slur against those that practised the art of witchcraft. Some of the ingredients would have been incredibly toxic and produced a hallucinogenic affect. The chemicals in a number of the herbs mentioned would have produced psychoactive and/or sedative effects.

Gerald Gardner includes a recipe in his Gardnerian Book of Shadows that includes lard, hashish, hemp flower, poppy flower, powdered hellebore root and ground sunflower seed. With the instructions to rub the mixture behind the ears, on the neck, under the armpits, to the left of the sympathetic nerve, behind the knees, on the soles of the feet and inside your elbows. You should then sleep naked in front of a fire or a statue of the goddess.

From Margaret Murray's The Witch-Cult in Western Europe we are given three French recipes which include: Parsley, water of aconite, poplar leaves and soot, or, Water parsnip, sweet flag, cinquefoil, bat's blood, deadly nightshade and oil, or, Baby's fat, juice of water parsnip, aconite, cinquefoil, deadly nightshade and soot.

> ¹"There take this unbaptised brat,
> Boil it well; preserve the fat:
> You know 'tis precious to transfer
> Our 'nointed flesh into the air
> In moonlight nights,
> I thrust in eleoselinum lately,

1   The Discoverie of Witchcraft, Reginald Scott, 1584

Aconitum, frondes populeas and soot—
Then sium, acorum vulgare too,
Pentaphyllon, the blood of a flitter-mouse
Solanum somnificum et oleum.
When hundred leagues in the air, we feast and sing,
Dance, kiss, and coll, use everything:
What young man can we wish to pleasure us,
But we enjoy him in an incubus.'

Here is a breakdown on the most popular ingredients and my thoughts on working with them today and possible substitutions. I would not recommend creating or working with any of the old recipes, most of them include very toxic items that would be potentially dangerous to you and your health. However, there are some that can still be used and modern alternatives that won't get you killed, maimed or arrested. Some of these are used in homeopathic medicine but, and here is the important part, they should only be prescribed by a qualified herbalist that has taken into account any medical history or mediations. Never self-diagnose or self-prescribe. I have erred on the side of caution here.

You could make flying ointments to add to your pulse points or an essential oil blend for anointing your third eye. Alternatively, you could create an incense blend or herbal tea to help you journey. Experiment and have fun with your creations, if it doesn't smell or taste right on the first attempt tweak it or create a new one for next time. Herbs I would NOT recommend using for flying ointment, generally all parts of the following plants are dangerous. Most of them could be used in spell work such as adding to witch bottles or spell pouches. However, applying to the skin or ingesting, in my humble opinion is really not worth the risk. They have so many medical warnings, could cause adverse health effects, even fatal ones and could react badly with medical conditions or medications.

Aconite (Aconitum spp) (also covers wolfsbane)
Belladonna (Atropa belladonna) - Belladonna also known as Deadly Nightshade
Datura (Datura stramonium)
Hemlock (Conium maculatum)
Henbane (Hyoscyamus niger)
Mandrake (Mandragora offcinale)

Babies

It goes without saying no part of any babies should not be added to flying ointment. If you need fat then lard, oil or bees/soy wax is a much better alternative. My herb suggestions for use in flying ointments, oils and incense blends.

Almond
(Prunus dulcis)

Use the flowers, leaves, wood or oil. Almond nut shells also work well for magical use. Almond Magical Properties: Love, prosperity, treasure, intuition, psychic powers, passion

Apple
(Malus spp)

Use the flowers, leaves, pips and wood or essential oil. Apple slices or peel can be dried in a low oven. Apple Magical Properties: Love, healing, clarity, knowledge, abundance, spirit work

Cinnamon
(Cinnamomum zeylanicum, Cinnamomum verum)

Use cinnamon sticks or cassia bark pieces or ground cinnamon or the essential oil. Cinnamon Magical Properties: Success, healing, power, psychic powers, protection, love, focus, lust, spirituality, changes

Cinquefoil
(Potentilla spp)

Cinquefoil brings the magic of dreams, divination and protection. Use: The flowers and leaves or as an essential oil. Cinquefoil magical properties: Luck, prosperity, protection, good fortune, dispel negative energy, balance, fairy magic, purification, dreams

Fat

The original flying ointments although stated they used babies' fat; it was more likely to have been lard or beef dripping used as a base for the other ingredients. I would recommend a mixture of oil and bees or soy wax to create a balm, but lard could be used if you prefer the authentic grease.

Grapefruit
(Citrus paradise)

Use the flowers, leaves, wood or pips. Grapefruit slices or peel can be dried in a low oven. Grapefruit can also be used as an essential oil.

Grapefruit Magical Properties: Happiness, spirit work, purification, depression, energy

Heather
(Calluna spp, Erica spp, vulgaris)

Use the flowers and leaves. Heather Magical Properties: Luck, protection, cleansing, ghosts, rain, spirit, love, friendship, faeries, dreams, shape shifting

Jasmine
(Jasminum grandiflorum, Jasminum officinale, Jasminum odoratissimum)

Use the flowers and leaves or essential oil. Jasmine Magical Properties: Dreams, money, love, meditation, lust

Marigold
(Calendula officinalis)

Use the flowers, leaves and root of the plant or essential oil. Marigold Magical Properties: Psychic powers, dreams, protection, luck, happiness, gossip

Mugwort
(Artemisia vulgaris)

Collect the flowers when they are open or just before and use the leaves as well, it can also be used in essential oil form. Mugwort Magical Properties: Strength, psychic powers, protection, dreams, healing, astral travel, feminine energy, cleansing

Poppy
(Papaver spp)

The species of poppy used for opiates and the sedative properties is the papaver somniferum (translates as sleep bringing). They also provide the poppy seeds and poppy seed oil we use for culinary purpose. Whilst the seeds and oil won't produce a narcotic effect, they can be used for magical purpose. Poppy Magical Properties: Love, sleep, money, luck, fertility, rebirth, grief

Rose (Rosa spp)

Use the petals, leaves and thorns or essential oil. Rose Magical Properties: Love, psychic powers, healing, luck, protection, peace, mysteries, knowledge, dreams, friendship, death and rebirth, abundance

Star Anise (Illicum verum)

Use the dried star shape spices or essential oil. Star Anise Magical Properties: Luck, psychic powers, purification, protection, dreams, spirituality, sleep

Wormwood (Artemisia absinthium)

Use the leaves and as an essential oil. Wormwood Magical Properties: Vengeance, attack magic, protection, divination, dreams, meditation, psychic powers

Yarrow (Achillea millefolium)

Use the flowers, leaves and stems or essential oil. Yarrow Magical Properties: Psychic powers, love, courage, exorcism, dreams, peace, happiness, divination, protection.

Flying Ointment Balm

This balm can be used to rub on your pulse points (wrists and temples) to impart the magic to help you hedge ride.

Basic recipe:
56g/2oz base oil such as almond, coconut or grapeseed
28g/1oz beeswax or soy wax
20 drops of your chosen essential oils

Melt your base oil and beeswax slowly over a double boiler, stirring occasionally with a wooden spoon. When the beeswax is completely melted, add the essential oils, stir, and immediately pour carefully into tins/jars. Leave to cool completely for several hours, then pop on lids.

Flying Oil Blend

Use to anoint your pulse points and your third eye before hedge riding. Oil blends can also be added to an oil burner, I pop a piece of wax into the top first then add the oil, it stops it from burning. Please test a drop or two on a small area of your skin before you go slapping on loads of oil, just in case you are allergic to it. NEVER put essential oil straight onto your skin, always mix it into a base oil first. For a blend to use in an oil burner, bath or diffuser you can create a blend without using a base oil. Any blend you are intending to use on your skin for anointing or massage NEEDS to be diluted with a base oil.

Basic recipe:
10ml base oil
20-25 drops essential oil

My suggestions for either the ointment balm or oil blend: I like to use almond oil as the base because it carries the magical properties of boosting your intuition and psychic abilities.

5 drops wormwood essential oil
5 drops rose essential oil
5 drops mugwort essential oil
5 drops yarrow essential oil

Or

5 drops cinquefoil essential oil
10 drops jasmine essential oil
5 drops cinnamon essential oil
5 marigold essential oil

33
Hedge Riding Herbal Tea

You can use bought herbal tea bags or you can make your own. Herbal tea can be drunk hot or left to cool and served over ice. Work with fresh or dried herbs or mix and match herbal tea bags.

As a general rule use one or two teaspoons of the dried herb mix, pour on hot water and brew for at least 5 minutes then strain. If you are using fresh herbs you may need to add a larger quantity. If you prefer you can use your regular black tea as a base and add in other herbals. NOTE: Please be careful and make sure you have identified the herb correctly. Never ingest herbs that you aren't sure about. Always check with a qualified practitioner if you are on medication, have health problems or are pregnant.

Herbal teas can be a bit bitter and often no matter what blend you go with; in my opinion they taste like grass. I like to add a spoonful of honey to my blends to sweeten them. If you purchase ready-made blends or herbal tea bags do make sure to check the ingredients list, a lot of the big brand names put 'fillers' in and you end up with more 'sweepings from the factory floor' than you do the supposed main flavour.

My suggestions:
Black tea base with a few fresh blackberries
Black tea base with mugwort and rose petals
Dandelion root coffee with a pinch of cinnamon
Nettle tea with a spoonful of honey and a slice of apple
Dried apple pieces steeped with a star anise and a pinch of cinnamon
Dried yarrow and dried elderberries
Dried yarrow, dried elderberries and dried hawthorn berries
Dried mugwort, yarrow and cinnamon

34
Hedge Riding Candle

When I hedge ride, I like to begin by lighting a candle, it not only helps to set the scene but also gives me a focus to begin my descent. I keep a large pillar candle or sometimes a taper candle that has been dedicated for the purpose of hedge riding. Here is how I create mine:

You will need:

A pillar or taper/dinner candle, I like to work with a black candle.
Almond oil
A loose incense blend, I use the same ingredients as I do for my hedge riding incense blend but crush them until they are a fine powder.

Dress the candle with the almond oil, draw the oil from the top down to the centre of the candle and then from the bottom up to the centre. Next tip a layer of your ground incense blend onto a chopping board or tray then roll your candle in it. You might have to sprinkle some onto the candle and pat it down to make it stick well. Then your candle is dressed, at this point I like to dedicate it by saying:

Candlelight, magic of fire and flame
Show me the way to the other worlds
Guide me into the other realms

And keep me safe
Make it so

Pop the candle in a safe holder and this can be lit each time you jump the hedge and snuffed out afterwards. Then reused next time you take a journey. When my candle is on the last little bit of life, I light a new candle from the flame of the old one. This helps to pass the hedge riding energy over to a new candle. I have chosen ingredients that I have in my kitchen cupboards that are associated with Otherworld connection, but you may prefer to just use ingredients that relate to the hedgerow and grow in your local area.

35
Crystals

[1]"Seven kinds and ten of Jasper stones
reported are to be,
Of manie colours this is knowne
which noted is by me,
And said in manie places of
the world for to be seene,
Where it is bred; but yet the best
is thorough shining greene,
And that which prooved is to have
in it more virtue plaste:
For being borne about of such
as are of living chaste,
It drives awaie their ague fits,
the dropsie thirsting drie,
And put unto a woman weake
in travell which dooth lie
It helps, assists, and comforts hir
in pangs when she dooth crie.
Againe, it is beleevd to be
A safegard franke and free,
To such as weare and beare the same;

---

1   The Discoverie of Witchcraft, Reginald Scott, 1584

and if it hallowed bee
It makes the parties gratious,
and mightie too that have it,
And noysome fansies (as they write
that ment not to deprave it)
It dooth displace out of the mind:
the force thereof is stronger,
In silver if the same be set,
and will endure the longer.'

Just as there are many herbals that can assist in hedge riding, there are also crystals that hold the same magical properties. I like to add one or two to my journey pouch, but you can use them to hold in your hand or place in the area you are going to be working in. You only need a small tumble stone size crystal to be able to connect with the magical energies. If you have a piece of jewellery with a stone set in that can be used as well, it will bring the added energy from the metal setting.

Charging your crystal

When you work with a crystal you will need to give it instructions on what you require from it. Be polite, but make sure you really push your intent into the stone. Hold the crystal in the palm of your hand and ask it to be your guardian and gateway to the Otherworld. You may want to pass the crystal through some incense smoke or anoint it with a flying ointment oil blend as well. Once you are done with the crystal you can cleanse it and re-use again.

Amber

Technically not a crystal, amber is fossilised resin which makes it incredibly ancient and gives a good strong link for hedge riding. Amber magical properties: Manifesting, energy, beauty, sun magic, power, wishes, intellect, clarity, wisdom, balance, purification, protection, psychic abilities, healing, calm, patience, love, sensuality, good luck, marriage, abundance, success, vitality, joy, sexuality, cleansing, stress, harmony, creativity.

Aventurine (green)

Although it comes in other colours, aventurine is commonly green and is a variety of quartz. Aventurine (green) magical properties: Balance, decisions, motivation, leadership, dreams, visualisation, creativity, luck, money, anxiety, calm, opportunities, happiness, adventure, love, courage, truth, comfort, support, healing, peace, connection, perception, intellect, psychic abilities.

Celestite

The name celestite is from Latin and translates as 'heavenly or celestial', perfect for any kind of connection to the divine or Otherworld. Celestite magical properties: Divine, spirit work, love, clarity, decisions, meditation, communication, peace, dreams, stress, healing, astral travel, calming, uplifting, harmony, happiness, spirituality.

Chrysocolla

Ancient Egyptians referred to chrysocolla as the 'wise stone of conciliation' which makes it a very clever and wise stone indeed.

Chrysocolla magical properties: Wisdom, peace, patience, love, soothing, intuition, energy, calming, emotions, fear, strength, clarity, balance, negative energy, insight, releasing, spirituality, psychic abilities, guilt, divine, harmony, communication, meditation

Citrine

Another crystal from the quartz family, often used throughout history as a talisman against evil, so it brings a nice protective energy when journeying.

Citrine magical properties: Happiness, joy, sun magic, negative energy, optimism, abundance, depression, stress, success, wealth, healing, intuition, creativity, confidence, changes, self-esteem, protection, psychic powers, fears, clarity, stamina, nightmares

Garnet

The name garnet may come from the Latin word 'granatus' which means pomegranate. Perfect for travelling to the Underworld!

Garnet magical properties: Organisation, warrior spirit, protection, love, commitment, passion, sexuality, sensuality, attraction, depression, spiritual healing, success, self-confidence, energy, inspiration, perception, strength, survival, fear, courage, clarity, challenges, past life work, truth, compassion, deflecting negative energy, gossip, ambition, motivation, goals, purification, cleansing, balance, inner strength, self-empowerment, creativity, confidence, meditation, spirit work, nightmares, journeying, abundance, support

Howlite

Howlite is naturally white with grey and black veins, if you find a coloured stone it will have been dyed. It is the veins in the stone that I think link it so well to journeying.

Howlite magical properties: Understanding, wisdom, connection, truth, meditation, focus, stress, anxiety, calm, strength, peace, releasing, emotions, selfishness, communication, creativity, inspiration, motivation, concentration, support, patience, relaxation, courage, past life work, astral travel

Kyanite

Kyanite has a beautiful blue colour with a pearly sheen, there is something very tranquil and dream like about this stone. Kyanite magical properties: Balance, harmony, calming, connection, psychic abilities, healing, communication, grounding, transformation, meditation, relaxation, luck, growth, leadership, new beginnings, clarity, decisions, stability, truth, vitality, abundance, spirituality, channelling, understanding, dreams

Labradorite

Labradorite has a similar structure to moonstone, but it has a darker, deeper more inner work kind of energy. Labradorite magical properties: Transformation, cleansing, breaking patterns, potential, psychic abilities, intuition, confidence, spirituality, focus, protection, imagination, relaxation, soothing, energy, healing, stress, anxiety, luck, abundance, success, decisions, trust, changes, strength, courage, self-confidence, inspiration, perseverance, journeying, clarity, insight, meditation, depression, jealousy, grounding

Lepidolite

Lepidolite is a beautiful purple, pink stone that often has crystal lines running through it, pretty and practical for spiritual journeying. Lepidolite magical properties: Transformation, soothing, calming, stress, happiness, changes, emotions, psychic abilities, spirituality, depression, divination, connection, strength, uplifting, luck, hope, balance, peace, sleep, harmony, decisions, addiction, releasing, trust, goals, optimism, patience, dreams, opportunities, support, love

Malachite

Malachite is a gorgeous green stone with bands of different shades of green running through it. The green is caused by copper which is an excellent metal for conducting energy which makes it fabulous to work with. Malachite magical properties: Changes, transformation, clarity, emotions, protection, support, healing, peace, travel, fears, growth, creativity, renewal, energy, wealth, money, opportunity, abundance, new beginnings, finances, success, business, focus, strength, wisdom, releasing, prosperity, breaking barriers, psychic abilities, manifestation, soothing, stress, love, power.

Moonstone

Moonstone is the lighter cousin of labradorite and with its strong connections to the moon it makes a lovely stone to work with for magic. Moonstone magical properties: New beginnings, moon magic, intuition, calming, psychic abilities, balance, harmony, wishes, cleansing, uplifting, hope, meditation, emotions, love, divination, spirituality, wealth, truth, healing, sensuality, insight, peace, wisdom, communication, confidence, abundance, prosperity, dreams, fertility, travel

Obsidian (black)

Black obsidian is the heavy metal rock god of the crystal world bringing in the energy of volcanic lava. It brings together the magic of fire, earth and water. Obsidian magical properties: Truth, healing, clarity, illusions, breaking barriers, integrity, grounding, centring, strength, courage, protection, cleansing, meditation, stress, calming, relaxation, depression, anxiety, wealth, luck, focus, emotions, power, determination, success, patience, perseverance, releasing, spirit work, spirituality, challenges, past life work, divination

Pebble/Hag Stone

This is the easiest and cheapest (as in, free) stone to work with for hedge riding and that is an ordinary pebble. If you can find a hag stone, even better. Hag stones are pebbles with a hole in, the hole is created naturally by water which is why you will find the holey stones near the sea or river. Pebbles combine all the elements, they come from the earth, they have sat in the sun, the rain or river/sea water and experienced the air. Pebble/hag stone magical properties: Protection, fairy magic, nightmares, dreams, healing, fertility, manifestation, negative energy

Pyrite

Pyrite gets its name from the Greek 'pyr' which translates to mean 'fire'. It is sparkly and shiny and often referred to as 'fool's gold', but a fool it certainly is not.

Pyrite magical properties:Releasing, breaking patterns, clarity, protection, support, decisions, growth, success, inspiration, grounding, vitality, learning, perception, memory, wisdom, psychic abilities, healing, cleansing, prosperity, wealth, abundance, luck, strength, motivation, manifestation, finances, energy, sun magic, power, focus, perseverance, confidence, divination, communication, self-confidence, meditation

Quartz (clear)

Clear quartz is a good general 'all-rounder' kinda crystal to work with. If you only ever purchase one crystal, make it this one, as it is a multi-tasker that also works to cleanse other crystals too.

Quartz magical properties: Purification, cleansing, healing, calming, emotions, strength, support, spirituality, energy, balance, psychic abilities, motivation, uplifting, decisions, anxiety, divine connection, amplifying, focus, meditation, manifestation, channelling, protection, negative energy, clarity, wisdom, concentration, learning, spirit work, communication, astral travel, divination, dreams, harmony

Rhodonite

Beautiful shades of pink and rose with dark veins running through which for me, makes rhodonite a perfect choice for travelling through the Otherworld.

Rhodonite magical properties: Protection, renewal, emotions, strength, soothing, clarity, happiness, love, balance, harmony, decisions, confidence, spirituality, peace, energy, passion, optimism, changes, vitality, anxiety, travel, psychic abilities, self-confidence, trust, calming, relaxation, patience, determination, releasing, stress, negative energy

Selenite

Selenite is possibly one of the most spiritual crystals to work with, it has a direct connection to all things Otherworldly.

Selenite magical properties: Clarity, psychic protection, cleansing, balance, stability, emotions, divine, connections, spirituality, psychic abilities, spirit work, protection, healing, breaking barriers, decisions, intuition, meditation, money, success, love

Silver

I know it isn't a crystal, but metals have magical properties too and silver has a good conductive quality.

Silver magical properties: Healing, communication, cleansing, energy, intuition, stability, spirituality, patience, perseverance, moon magic, negative energy, protection, balance, psychic abilities, manifestation, wealth, prosperity, abundance, travel, dreams, emotions, purification, love, peace, astral travel

Sodalite

Sodalite is a stone often favoured by artists and creators, it is a stunning blue colour and comes with shots of white specks and streaks running through it.

Sodalite magical properties: Creativity, communication, peace, friendship, clarity, truth, connection, knowledge, wisdom, emotions, balance, divination, psychic abilities, cleansing, confidence, fears, love, intuition, decisions, perseverance, anxiety, insight, organisation, self-esteem, releasing, understanding, harmony, learning, dreams, meditation

Sugilite

Sugilite is the most amazing purple colour which positively shouts 'spiritual vibes baby!'.

Sugilite magical properties: Spirituality, wisdom, clarity, insight, courage, truth, passion, inspiration, healing, strength, channelling, psychic abilities, amplification, confidence, focus, love, emotions, releasing, calming, peace, protection, connection, balance, understanding, stress

Tiger's Eye

Tiger's eye...looks like a tiger's eye or perhaps a cat eye, definitely one of the feline family anyway. Being an eye, it is 'all seeing'.

Tiger's eye magical properties: Amplification, balance, harmony, releasing, fears, anxiety, courage, strength, self-confidence, focus, creativity, optimism, self-worth, protection, psychic abilities, healing, wealth, money, opportunity, abundance, prosperity, luck, success, commitment, determination, support, clarity, vitality, motivation, grounding, patience

Tourmaline

Ancient Egyptians believed tourmaline travelled from the core of the earth, along a rainbow and up towards the sun, thereby explaining all the colours this crystal comes in.

Tourmaline magical properties: Calming, harmony, balance, insight, spirituality, protection, negative energy, transformation, courage, grounding, fears, creativity, understanding, power, motivation, commitment, patience, stability, releasing, emotions, anxiety, strength, happiness, protection, relaxation, friendship, astral travel

Turquoise

Turquoise has been worn and treasured for centuries, in fact longer than that.

Turquoise magical properties: Purification, negative energy, protection, balance, relaxation, emotions, stress, spirituality, energy, depression, clarity, wisdom, understanding, psychic abilities, insight, intuition, past life work, communication, wealth, abundance, finances, prosperity, luck, decisions, friendship, uplifting, meditation, love, harmony

36
Park your broomstick

Once you have learnt the ropes and jumped on your broomstick, flown over the hedge and into the Otherworld you will have begun the most amazing journey. It is an incredible skill to have and can provide so much insight and knowledge that you might not otherwise have access to. It can be tempting to leave one foot on the other side, but this can lead to all sorts of complications in daily life. As long as you remember to be respectful and sensible, hedge riding is safe and quite possibly one of the most wonderful journeys to take.

Recommended Reading

Craft of the Hedge Witch – Smythe, Geraldine, 2022
Treading the Mill – Nigel G Pearson, 2017
Leechcraft, Early English Charms, Plant lore and Healing – Stephen Pollington, 2000
Folk Magic, Superstition and Charms, Carl Marwick, 2020
Flower Lore and Legend, Katharine M Beals, 1917
Discovering the Folklore of Plants, Margaret Baker, 1969
Hedgerow Medicine, Julie Bruton-Seal and Matthew Seal, 2008
A Broom at Midnight, Roger J Horne, 2021
Folk Witchcraft, Roger J Horne, 2019
Witch's Garden, Sandra Lawrence, 2020
Culpeper's Complete Herbal/The English Physitian, Nicholas Culpeper (circa 17th Century)
Pantheon The Norse, Morgan Daimler, 2022
The Greek Magical Papyri in Translation, Including the Demotic Spells: Texts v. 1, Hans Dieter Betz (Editor), 1997
The Witch's Art of Incantation, Roger J Horne, 2021
Carmina Gadelica, Alexander Carmichael, 1909

About the Author

I am an English witch who has been walking the Pagan pathway for over thirty years. A working wife and mother who has been lucky enough to have had over 25 books published (so far), some of them becoming best sellers. My passion is to learn, I love to study and have done so from books, online resources, schools and wonderful mentors over the years and still continue to learn each and every day, but I have learnt the most from actually getting outside and doing it.

I like to laugh ... and eat cake...

It is my pleasure to give talks to pagan groups and co-run open rituals and workshops run by the Kitchen Witch Coven. I am also High Priestess of the Kitchen Witch Coven and an Elder at the on-line Kitchen Witch School of Natural Witchcraft. I am host of the Pagan Portals Podcast, which can be found on all the usual podcast platforms. A regular columnist with Fate & Fortune magazine, I also contribute articles to several magazines such as Pagan Dawn and Witchcraft & Wicca. You will find my regular ramblings on my own personal blog and YouTube channel. My craft is a combination of old religion witchcraft, Wicca, hedge witchery, kitchen witchery and folk magic. My heart is that of an English Kitchen Witch.

It was my honour to be added to the Watkins 'Spiritual 100 List' for 2023.

www.rachelpatterson.co.uk
facebook.com/rachelpattersonbooks
www.kitchenwitchhearth.net
facebook.com/kitchenwitchuk
Email: HQ@kitchenwitchhearth.net
www.youtube.com/user/Kitchenwitchuk
www.instagram.com/racheltansypatterson

MY BOOKS
Moon Books
Spells & Charms
Garden Magic
Crystal Magic
The Element of Earth
The Element of Fire
The Element of Water
The Art of Ritual
Beneath the Moon
Witchcraft ... into the Wilds
Grimoire of a Kitchen Witch
A Kitchen Witch's World of Magical Foods
A Kitchen Witch's World of Magical Plants & Herbs
Arc of the Goddess (co-written with Tracey Roberts)
Moon Books Gods & Goddesses Colouring Book (Patterson family)
Practically Pagan: An Alternative Guide to Cooking

Pagan Portals:
Kitchen Witchcraft
Hoodoo Folk Magic
Moon Magic
Meditation
The Cailleach
Animal Magic
Sun Magic
Triple Goddess
Gods & Goddesses of England
Dragon Magic
Sulis

Llewellyn
Curative Magic
A Witch for All Seasons: Spells, Rituals, Festivals, and Magic
Practical Candle Magic: Witchcraft with Wick & Wax

Solarus
Flower Magic Oracle Deck

Animal Dreaming Publishing
Magical Herbs Oracle Deck part of the Kitchen Witch series

www.ingramcontent.com/pod-product-compliance
Lightning Source LLC
Chambersburg PA
CBHW050417120526
44590CB00015B/1996